HIGHLAND RAILWAY LIVERIES

HOWARD GEDDES & EDDIE BELLASS
WITH PETER TATLOW
HIGHLAND RAILWAY SOCIETY

Duke class built in 1883 at Lochgorm No. 71 *Clachnacuddin*, in Peter Drummond's fully lined-out livery with the full company name on the tender. Note that the emergency gong on the tender side is missing, although the rest of the gear appears to be in place. *[RK Blencowe collection*

PENDRAGON

IN ASSOCIATION WITH

Frontispiece. Obtained from Dübs in 1892 as the result of a cancelled order for the Uruguay Eastern Rly., No. 101 and her sister No. 102 were so successful in service that the Highland ordered a further 3 locomotives in 1893. They were known (somewhat inaccurately) as the Yankee Tanks. No. 101 was originally named *Olmos* after a Uruguayan town. No. 101 is standing on the turntable at Inverness, looking extremely shiny and clean in 1913, in Drummond's simple style of livery, accompanied by those responsible for her sparkling appearance.

[L&GRP 7882

The Title. The Gaelic *Dathan na Gaidhealtachd* is literally translated as "Colours of the Highlands". It is pronounced "d-an na glt'-achg". Although there is no record of the Highland Railway Co. ever using the Gaelic in the course of business, the Company served an area of the country where Gaelic was the primary language, even into living memory, and it seems appropriate to recognise this in this small way.

HIGHLAND RAILWAY LIVERIES

Dàthan na Gaidhealtachd

HOWARD GEDDES & EDDIE BELLASS
WITH PETER TATLOW
HIGHLAND RAILWAY SOCIETY

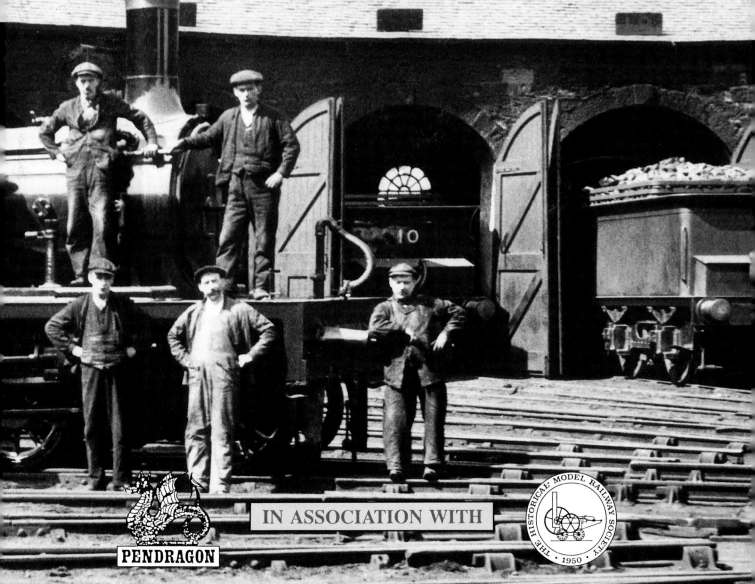

PENDRAGON

IN ASSOCIATION WITH

THE HISTORICAL MODEL RAILWAY SOCIETY · 1950

From: The Rt. Hon. The Viscount Whitelaw. K.T.. C.H., M.C.

HOUSE OF LORDS
LONDON SW1A 0PW

4th July, 1995

I am delighted to have been asked to give a short foreword for
the Highland Railway Society.

This is particularly interesting for me because my grandfather,
William Whitelaw, was Chairman of the Highland Railway before
he later became Chairman of the North British Railway and the
LNER in turn.   He gave his life to the railways and, in
particular, was proud of what had happened in the Highland
Railway.

I spent my life as a boy at Nairn, and so was taught all about
the Highland Railway at that time.   I wish your Society every
possible success.

© Highland Railway Society, Historical Model Railway Society and The Pendragon Partnership 1995

Published by The Pendragon Partnership, PO Box No. 3, Easingwold, York, YO6 3YS
All rights reserved

Typesetting and Page Layout: Howard Geddes

Jacket and Supplementary Design by Barry C. Lane, Sutton-in-Craven

Print and Repro: The Amadeus Press Ltd., Huddersfield, West Yorkshire

British Cataloguing-in-Publication Data: a catalogue reference for this book is held by the British Library

ISBN No. 1 899816 02 X

*Note: The publishers and authors regret that copies of photographs and drawings appearing in this book
cannot be made available to readers*

CONTENTS

INTRODUCTION

This book has its origins in four duplicated data sheets compiled by Sir Eric Hutchison and Gavin L Wilson in 1950.

In the mid-1970s, several articles and drawings by Eddie Bellass describing Highland Railway locomotives appeared in the *Model Railway Constructor*. Much important information was received during the following correspondence, with locomotive and rolling stock liveries predominating.

With the kind permission and willing co-operation of Gavin Wilson, revision and expansion of the original data commenced in early 1976, drafts being circulated by Eddie Bellass to several railway and model railway enthusiasts known to be interested in the Highland Railway.

There things stood for some years. The formation of **The Highland Railway Society** in 1987 resulted in a new focus on the important subject of liveries. Eddie Bellass very kindly handed over existing material into the custodianship of the Society. Howard Geddes, on behalf of the Society, and with continuing input from Eddie Bellass, has undertaken the completion of *Highland Railway Liveries*, resulting in a considerable expansion of the material, bringing it to a form suitable for publication. *Highland Railway Liveries* is now available to as wide an audience as possible.

OBJECTIVE AND AIMS

The objective of *Highland Railway Liveries* is to record details of the various styles of livery and insignia applied by the Highland Railway and its predecessors to their significant and enduring assets.

Its aims are:-
* to be of interest to the historian;
* to assist in dating and identifying photographs, drawings and other historical records; and
* to enable modellers and others reproduce accurately these aspects of the Highland Railway.

Highland Railway Liveries is not intended to give a complete chronology of changes and deviations applied to individual items of rolling stock. However, with such small numbers of vehicles in any one class (especially locomotives), references to individual cases do occur.

Within its scope, *Highland Railway Liveries* is intended to be definitive.

STRUCTURE AND SCOPE

Highland Railway Liveries has been organised into tables as far as possible, with supporting text. Drawings have been provided where appropriate. Photographs have been chosen for their reference value and thus some are likely to have been published already, although a conscious attempt has been made to include less well-known photographs. Captions include a reference to the negative number where known. Carriage and wagon Diagram numbers are those introduced by DLG Hunter: whilst they are not quite the same as the "official" ones, they are generally accepted nowadays as the standard for identification and reference purposes.

The livery and insignia of an object assist an observer in identifying its ownership. There are other characteristics which achieve the same aim but whose design, arrangement and usage are not included in *Highland Railway Liveries*: marks on company assets (e.g. an "H R" stamped on cutlery), company seals, design of stationery, letter headings, tickets, luggage labels, timetables and other ephemera, style of uniforms, and so on. Apart from the current scarcity of information, these topics are incidental to the objective of *Highland Railway Liveries*; perhaps they will be addressed another day.

However, train lamps and boards are included, since their presence on a train is obvious and their positioning on a locomotive and their usage is unique to the Highland. Lamp irons on locomotives are also discussed, since their style and positioning are intimately linked with the lamps themselves.

Particular attention has been given to manufacturers' works plates, even though they were not specific to the Highland of course. Their inclusion is justifiable as they are part and parcel of a locomotive's insignia.

Although Private Trader wagons that ran regularly from foreign stations are not covered, those where their home station was on the Highland system have been included.

Foreign stock running on Highland lines (e.g. West Coast Joint Stock) is not covered - there are other reference sources.

The geographic scope of *Highland Railway Liveries* covers the natural territory of the Highland Company, being all the lines that the Highland owned or operated, including the Dornoch and Lybster Light Railways, but excluding the Invergarry and Fort Augustus Railway which the Highland only operated for a short period and which is more naturally associated with the West Highland and North British Railways.

Highland Railway Liveries would not be complete without an overview of the application of standard LMS and even BR liveries to Highland locomotives, rolling stock and lineside equipment. This Chapter has been contributed by Peter Tatlow, member of both the Highland Railway and the LMS Societies.

CHAPTER 1 - LOCOMOTIVE LIVERY AND INSIGNIA

THE EARLIEST DAYS - WILLIAM BARCLAY (1855-1865)

The man who arguably could be regarded as the father of The Highland Railway, the man whose vision and ability enabled the Highlands literally to have an efficient line of communication with the south, rather than the southrons reaching the Highlands, was Joseph Mitchell. His life has been chronicled elsewhere; his influence was pervasive. [1]

It was he who recommended that Alexander Allan, then Locomotive Superintendent of the Scottish Central Railway, design and supervise the supply of the initial motive power. In turn, Allan had his nephew William Barclay appointed Locomotive Superintendent.

William Barclay was thus the first person nominally responsible for the locomotives' livery, of all the antecedent companies of the Highland. He was responsible for the running and maintenance of the locomotives, not their design nor supply. Hence, Barclay simply maintained his engines in the livery in which they had been supplied: basically all-over dark green with black borders and boiler/firebox bands.

The boiler/firebox bands might have been lined thin red, but there are references which state there was no thin lining. There were black-bordered panels, the borders having incurved (concave) corners: two larger panels on the main tender side, one smaller on the tender cab side and three medium ones on the locomotive cab side - these can just be made out in Plate 1.

Few details are known, but it has been stated that the names of the very first locomotives - four 'Raigmore' Class 2-2-2s - were on narrow curved brass plates on the splasher; [2] the numbers were on the buffer beam.

On 'Seafield' Class 2-4-0s Nos. 10 and 11, the running numbers "No (hook) nn" were painted gold,

Plate 1. 'Seafield' Class 2-4-0 No. 11 showing Barclay livery. The plate on the footplate frame is the works plate (Hawthorn & Co., Leith), not a name plate. Unnamed at first, No. 11 was soon named *Stafford*, even so carrying that name only for a short time, replacing the "I&AJRy" on the splasher. This was also true of No. 10 *Westhall*. The other locomotives of the class - Nos. 5 to 9 - were named from the start, described as having their names on the splasher on small curved brass nameplates, like Nos. 1-4. However, after a short time, they too became nameless. Presumably, the "I&AJRy" returned to the splashers in all cases. *[Real Photographs 4019*

---

[1]   Mitchell J, *Reminiscences Of My Life In The Highlands - Volumes 1 and 2*, reprinted David & Charles, 1971.

[2]   *The Locomotive*, 15th October 1915 pp 229-231. Note though that even these articles are half a century after the event. A Raigmore drawing in that article also appears in P Tatlow's *Highland Locomotives* and the RCTS Book I.

Plate 2. 'Belladrum' Class 2-2-2 No. 12 *Belladrum* itself, probably showing Stroudley's goods livery, but maybe Barclay's livery. The engine clearly bears a Highland Railway number plate. Since the engine lost its name around 1865, the photograph must be dated approximately mid to end 1865. Having been built in May 1862 for work by the I&AJR on the Inverness & Ross-shire Railway, it is possible that the engine still carries its original as-built livery.   *[HRS collection*

appearing only on the buffer beam, which was red; the "I. & A. J. RY." was also gold, on the splasher. It is likely that the rear buffer beam was also red, and it may be conjectured that the rear of the tender and the tool box also had incurved black bordered panels.

Plate 1 has appeared many times before, but is included here as the only known photograph of a locomotive definitely in I&AJR livery, and the only one with visible insignia of the Barclay regime. It may be conjectured that Nos. 5-9 were similarly identified.

The 'Small Goods (18)' and 'Medium Goods (36)' Class 2-4-0s were originally unnamed. The company initials and number appeared on the (front) splasher: "I & A J Ry No. nn", as evidenced in drawings of No. 21 and No. 36. [3] When named, the name plates were again curved brass replacing the company initials and number. The Sharp Stewart works plate was on the middle panel of the lower cab side, looking very similar to a number plate.

William Barclay continued in this role for each of the Highland's constituent companies, until just as the Inverness & Aberdeen Junction and Inverness & Perth Junction Railways were amalgamated on 1st February 1865, one of the Directors, struggling along with other passengers from a train whose engine had broken down, actually passed by Barclay who was fishing in a lineside pool, in working

hours! His fall from grace was swift: his services "would not be required after 31st May".

WILLIAM STROUDLEY (1865-1870)

Barclay was succeeded by William Stroudley, and almost immediately on 29th June 1865 the new company title was adopted: The Highland Railway.

It has been said that Stroudley continued with Barclay's livery for goods engines, but in reality he changed it fundamentally. The single body colour was replaced by a two-tone panelled livery, darker to the outside, lighter inside the panels. It is likely that the outer darker green was equivalent if not quite the same as Barclay's green - dark olive green or Brunswick Green would be a pragmatic description. The inner lighter green was probably olive green. Barclay's black lining was elaborated by edging it with white (inside) and red (outside). The panelling was extended to cover virtually the entire locomotive, there being some complicated curves and corners. Boiler bands remained black; they were elaborated by edging with a very thin red line on both sides, each flanked by a wider white line separated by a green band of the lighter body colour. See Plate 3.

This style of lining was taken by Stroudley to the London Brighton & South Coast Railway, where the green band is reliably described as olive green, corroborating the description of the Highland's

---

[3]   *The Locomotive,* 15 March 1916 pp 46-48. The No. 21 drawing also appears in P Tatlow's *Highland Locomotives* and No. 36 in C Hamilton Ellis' *Highland Engines and their Work,* Locomotive Publishing Co., 1930.

Plate 3. 'Rebuilt Raigmore' Class 2-4-0 No. 2 *Aldourie* showing Stroudley goods livery. William Stroudley is on the right in the cab, and Captain Wm. Fraser-Tytler (a director) is on the tender. Note the coloured coupling rod, and the Stroudley-style number plate on the cab-side, as well as the cab-side lining. *[Lens of Sutton 12377*

lighter body colour as olive green. On the LB&SC the outer colour for goods engines was black and for passenger dark olive green. It may be conjectured that either of these colours could have been applied to both goods and passenger engines on the Highland; indeed, the outer colour of the Barclay livery might have been black instead of or as well as dark green, although Plate 1 shows clearly a single overall dark green. On occasions the red lining was apparently omitted. Sometimes the inner lighter green body colour was used all over, substituting the outer darker green.

The corners of the lining seemed to vary somewhat, although this perception may be due to the differing quality of the surviving photographs rather than the reality. One style appears to be Inverted Corner or

even Inverted Loop - this can be detected in a photograph of rebuilt No. 1 *Raigmore*. Another photograph, this time of No. 12 *Belladrum* (see Plate 2), shows what appears to be a simpler Double Rounded Corner lining, whilst the second No. 2 *Aldourie* (see Plate 3) clearly has a more straightforward tightly radiused Rounded Corner lining. [4] Maybe there were other styles.

Not all Barclay goods engines were so re-liveried, but some passenger engines were. To further demonstrate that one cannot define a generic Stroudley style, a second photograph of No. 2 *Aldourie* [5] a few years on apparently in the same livery shows the tender with one panel, not two, and the cab-side number plate now with encircling lining. Furthermore, the coupling rod appears plain,

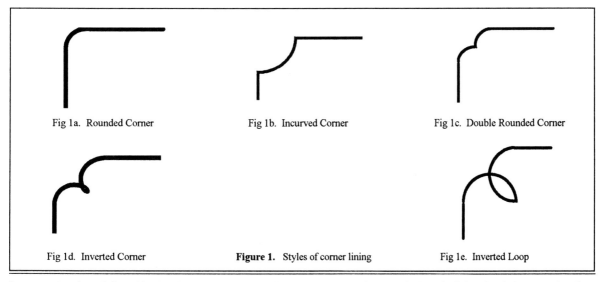

Fig 1a. Rounded Corner   Fig 1b. Incurved Corner   Fig 1c. Double Rounded Corner

Fig 1d. Inverted Corner   **Figure 1.** Styles of corner lining   Fig 1e. Inverted Loop

[4] See the *RCTS Highland Railway Locomotives Book I*, Figures 7, 14 and 8 respectively. The lining descriptions are taken from *Britain's Railway Liveries* by EF Carter - see Figure 1.
[5] *RCTS Highland Railway Locomotives Book I*, Figure 9.

whereas previously, as with sister-engine No. 1 *Raigmore*, the coupling rods were clearly coloured, although the colour itself is unknown.

Stroudley introduced his Improved Engine Green primarily for passenger classes, but some goods locomotives were also given the treatment. Stroudley is most remembered by the application of this famous colour to LB&SC locomotives, after his tenure of office at Inverness. But this peculiar shade had its origins on a line at the other end of the British Isles, and in fact was also known as Scotch Green.

Improved Engine Green was actually a dark yellow but with a hint of greenish hue in particular lights. It has also been described as a golden ochre - almost an orange ochre - that varied in tone according to changes in light and shade. The lining was the same as the goods version. Improved Engine Green was inside the lining, a darker ochre was outside (although the LB&SC version had dark olive green, which may also be true for the Highland). No photographs are known that show the Stroudley "yellow" livery on the Highland Railway. [6] In both goods and passenger liveries, smokeboxes, chimneys and tender axlebox horns were black; frames were claret, purportedly lined yellow and vermilion.

Although the Barclay locomotives had offered levels of weather-protection improving from a short weather-board on the first locomotives to a reasonable cab on the 'Belladrum' Class, Stroudley started to provide both passenger and goods locomotives with full cabs. Stroudley's cab roofs, which became so very familiar on the Brighton line, were very similar in shape to Barclay's. The cab roofs were white.

Stroudley also added cast brass number plates to the cab sides. These had polished numerals backed initially by yellow, then blue. See Figures 8 to 13 and Plate 3. It may be noted that the number plates were identical to those on the LB&SC, except that there the backing was always dark blue. It is possible that Barclay introduced these number plates shortly before Stroudley took over.

Stroudley decided to leave the Highland in January 1870 when the Directors felt unable to raise his salary to the figure being offered by the LB&SC.

Plate 4. 'Glenbarry' Class 2-4-0 No. 29 *Highlander* showing Jones I (1874) passenger livery. *[James Stevenson collection 82990]*

---

[6]   Obviously, the LB&SC may be taken as a reasonable reference, noting that at least two Stroudley liveried locomotives still exist, and there is an accurate model of Stroudley's 'D2' Class 0-4-2 No. 308 *Como* by Dr Bradbury Winter in the Brighton Museum and Art Gallery. For the record, Improved Engine Green was used for many years by the Netherlands Central Railway.

Plate 5. 'Big Goods' Class 4-6-0 No. 116 showing Jones II (1884) livery. Note the fish-scale effect produced by the final finishing off with an oily rag. *[Real Photographs*

DAVID JONES (1870-1896)

David Jones had joined the Inverness & Nairn Rly. soon after its opening in 1855, working first as an engine driver and then in 1858 as Assistant Locomotive Carriage & Wagon Superintendent under William Barclay. Having been passed over in favour of Stroudley, David Jones eventually achieved promotion to be in full charge of the Department, succeeding Stroudley from 25th January 1870. He continued the elaborate livery schemes until the first new engines built to his own design - the 'Duke' Class 4-4-0s - appeared in 1874.

Stroudley's main body colours (Improved Engine Green, dark ochre, olive green, dark olive green) were superseded or perhaps simply reformulated.

Thus, the 'Dukes' were painted in the revised passenger livery, with a new mid-green or light olive green with darker green borders and fully lined out in the Stroudley manner, except that the olive green part of the boiler band lining was changed to the new Jones mid-green. See Plate 4 for an example of the livery. One can only surmise what shade the outer green was.

Meanwhile, goods engines remained in either the dark green or even black livery, but repainting was done with a green that seemed to have a blue-ish tinge, a kind of dark bluey-green, described as "bluebottle". No photograph has been reliably identified of a locomotive painted in this livery.

Stroudley-style number plates were fitted to all engines as repainting took place, but with a vermilion background instead of blue.

From about 1884 two new shades of green were adopted for the main and secondary colours, apple green and olive green as described in Table 1, and all engines, new and overhauled, received this most elaborate and attractive finish, whether they were passenger or goods - Plates 5, 6 and 7 and Figure 3.

It has been stated that quite simply a new make of

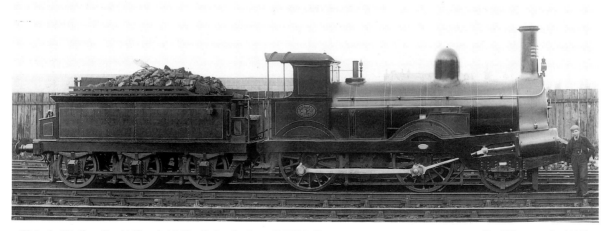

Plate 6. 'Medium Goods' Class 2-4-0 No. 42 showing Jones II (1884) livery. *[Real Photographs 14460*

Plate 7. 'Clyde Bogie' Class 4-4-0 No. 77 *Lovat* showing Jones II (1884) livery. Note the Jones style of number plate with the curly 77, and the Clyde Locomotive Co. works plate, where the works number No. 2 can be made out.

[NRM Tod collection 26

Plate 8. No. 123 *Loch Andorb*, looking extremely new, with no tablet catcher, although the cab roof is obviously not white. Note the lined-out tender-cab door, open and apparently secured with a length of rope. *[Ellis collection 12335*

paint was used which gave a much lighter finished shade (apple green); [7] when its performance was reported at a works sub-committee meeting, it was agreed to continue this shade for passenger engines.

Plate 8 shows the two-tone green very well. This and other photographs of Lochs when new or nearly new do seem to show a lighter apple green than other locomotives, but this may be simply differences in photographic technology rather than an intrinsic colour difference. Plate 9 has been included to show a 'Loch' in similar livery to *Loch Andorb*, but seemingly in traffic. And could that be Peter Drummond on the footplate? After all, he took over in November 1896 only two months after the

delivery of *Loch Maree*.

Further livery and lining details are shown in contemporary engravings in Figures 2 and 40, whilst Figure 23 shows some lining specifications for the 'Strath' Class 4-4-0s.

The lining of cab-sides of locomotives varied, but followed a logical pattern which depended upon the detail design of the cab-side and splashers, as follows:

- Barclay-style cab-sides which had horizontal seams, had two lined panels.
- Stroudley-style cab-sides with a cornered

Plate 9. No. 129 *Loch Maree*, showing Jones II livery, shortly after delivery and appearing to be in traffic, although still without a tablet catcher. *[Ellis collection 12930*

[7]   *Highland Railway Co. 1855-1955*, SLS, p59.

Plate 10. 'Barney' Class 0-6-0 No. 134 showing Drummond I fully-lined livery, with Drummond's first flat style of number plate. Note also the Dübs & Co. works plate, and the lining on the cab doors - for once closed.

[HRS collection

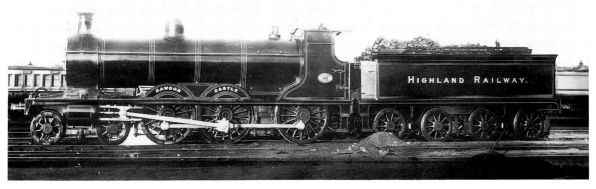

Plate 11. 'Castle' Class 4-6-0 No. 148 *Cawdor Castle*, showing Drummond I fully-lined livery. *[Real Photographs 44735]*

cab-front, had a single side-panel and a splasher-panel.

♦ Jones-style cab-sides with rounded corners had two side-panels and a splasher-panel. The 'Big Goods' Class 4-6-0s differed in design in the area of the splasher. Even though the cabs had rounded corners, the two panels did not go round the corner, and the small splasher panel was not extended onto the cab-side.

During his long years of office, Jones provided the Highland Railway with a fine stock of locomotives. When new they were often the most powerful of their era. Further, the locomotives were very robust on account of his retention of the Crewe-type double framing. All classes retained this feature except the

last two: the celebrated 'Big Goods' Class 4-6-0s of 1894 and the 'Loch' Class 4-4-0s of 1896.

Presumably as a safety measure, the 'Lochs' were the first HR locomotives to have tender-to-cab folding doors fitted as original equipment. Made of metal, they were in two parts, hinged to fold together, and attached with hinges to the tender. When in the closed position, they clipped over the outside of the engine cab's rear handrail. When in the open position, folded back against the tender, they were held in place by a simple latch - see Plate 28 - although a length of rope seemed to suffice on occasion - see Plate 8. These doors were usually left open, even on trains running at speed. The two parts of each door were lined as though a single panel, so that when folded open, only a rather

Plate 12. Rebuilt 'Glenbarry' Class 2-4-0 No. 55 *Invergordon* at Thurso in 1902, showing Drummond buffer beam insignia. No. 55 was built as a 2-2-2 in 1864 and named *Cluny*; rebuilt in 1874 and renamed *Sutherland*, it was renamed *Invergordon* in 1884, lasting until 1906 although its boiler survived on No. 42A (ex No. 37) until August 1923. Note the **THIRD** on the open door of the coupé coach next to the engine - see the Plate 37 for a surviving example. *[L&GRP 2378]*

Plate 13. 'Castle' Class 4-6-0 No. 146 *Skibo Castle*, showing Drummond II plain livery with the first style of number plate, on the turntable at Blair Atholl. The Dübs & Co. works plate is clearly visible on the smokebox saddle. Note the burnished smokebox door, and the signal wire post with a ladder, as well as the rare shot of some turntable detail.

[Peter Tatlow collection

curious half-panel was visible - see Plate 8.

At his retirement in 1896, enforced prematurely by a footplate accident, a large passenger 4-6-0 design was well advanced.

PETER DRUMMOND (1896-1912)

Peter Drummond found the main-line top-link locomotive stock adequate for immediate needs. He nonetheless completed Jones' work on the passenger 4-6-0 design, incorporating minor mechanical and major styling changes, including elder brother Dugald's patent steam-reversing mechanism. It duly appeared as the 'Castle' Class in 1900.

Drummond produced many other schemes for locomotives, some constructed and others rejected. All bore a remarkable likeness to the well established series evolved by brother Dugald for the North British, Caledonian and London & South Western Railways. He succeeded in introducing two more patent devices - the cross water-tube firebox and smokebox spark arrester - to a few examples of his own classes, but was refused permission to adopt his brother's feed water system, although the tenders which he designed had the necessary well already built into the tank bottoms. Drummond fitted wooden doors, hinged outwards from the tender, to most Jones engines except the 'Loch' Class 4-4-0s which had doors already.

Drummond's first change to the existing locomotive livery was to substitute the vermilion lines in the Jones style with a second white line - Figure 4 and Plates 10 and 11. The cab lining was continued similarly to Jones' three variations. Drummond's own design had a single cab-side panel. At the same time, he applied insignia to tender and tank sides and the engine number to front buffer beams - Plate 14. This identified the owning company more positively than the small indented title in the cab number plate.

There is photographic evidence showing that Drummond applied the insignia and numbers to some recently delivered or overhauled Jones' locomotives in Jones' livery without repainting them. For new engines of his own design, the cab number plates were themselves changed to a plain surfaced, flat type - see Figure 14. Locomotive running numbers were sometimes painted in 3 in. high numerals (white?) on the insides of the tender doors fitted by Drummond. Also, it is worth noting that the first engine to be allocated to the Dornoch Light Railway - 0-6-0T No. 56 *Dornoch* - had its running number painted on the rear cab sheet (there was no bunker fitted) whilst still lined out (see an atmospheric plate of The Mound station on page 83 of AJ Lambert's *Highland Railway Album I* - incidentally, this uniquely also shows the *rear* of a station nameboard).

The company insignia adopted comprised no less than three different styles - see Figure 5. These were introduced in quick succession and maintained concurrently throughout his lined and unlined periods.

A study of many contemporary photographs reveals

Plate 14. 'Small Ben' Class 4-4-0 No. 1 *Ben-y-Gloe* at Kyle of Lochalsh set up literally as a movie camera, showing Drummond buffer beam style with both the "HR" and "No." insignia. *[Ellis collection 17090*

Plate 15. 'Big Ben' Class 4-4-0 No. 68 *Ben A' Chait*, showing Drummond II plain livery, with later style of number plate. The North British Locomotive Co.'s works plate shows up well in this shot.

[HRS collection

Plate 16. 'Strath' Class 4-4-0 No. 100 *Glenbruar* at Kyle of Lochalsh, showing Drummond buffer beam style with just the "HR" insignia. Note the roof detail and the hanging lamp, also that the coupling link appears to be secured in the upright position with a length of wire. *[HRS collection*

a general lack of consistency in application, some classes having all three styles between them e.g. the 'Small Bens'. With only six engines in their class, the New or Large Bens managed to display all three styles between them. In one case, the same engine - No. 140 *Taymouth Castle* - showed both long styles in pictures taken only months apart.

In August 1902, the Highland Railway was well into a period of extreme financial constraint. One immediate casualty was the elaborate finish of the company's locomotive fleet. From that date, all lining-out was discontinued for repainting after overhaul and for new construction (note that manufacturers' posed photographs, in two-tone workshop grey with full lining, should be ignored). At the same time, a new shade of dark olive green was adopted and applied all over (except for traditionally black parts) even extending to the engine buffer beams. For a while some 4-4-0s, both tank and tender engines, were seen and photographed in service without the company title insignia, but this would appear to have been a temporary measure as the insignia re-appeared in later photographs of the same engines.

However, even in this new and plain livery, the engines were far from drab, thanks to the excellent

quality of the finish and also to the high standard of cleanliness which was maintained. See Plates 13 and 15.

Additionally, some minor but striking embellishments, devised and applied by individual locomotive and shed staff, ensured that the appearance of the locomotives met with approval from both the travelling public and the Highland Railway management, as confirmed by the use on Royal Trains of engines so treated. Some embellishments are described at the end of Table 2. See Plates 28 and 30. Plate 31 shows an example of temporary "embellishments", to illustrate just what apparitions might appear on the line from time to time.

With a few detailed variations covering the painting of minor parts and changes in the actual shade of green governed by availability of materials and mixing methods, the style adopted from 1902 was little changed for the rest of the Highland Railway Company's separate existence.

FREDERICK SMITH (1912-1915)

Frederick George Smith succeeded Drummond in February 1912, when the latter accepted a similar post on the Glasgow & South Western Railway. Smith had been Drummond's assistant as Works Manager, Inverness, since 1904, and prior to that had gained engineering experience in the North Eastern Railway, non-railway and electrical workshops. A great innovator, he modified the front end of the 1913 batch of 'Castles'; increased the

Plate 17. A none too sharp photo of 'Castle' Class 4-6-0 No. 144 *Blair Castle* leaving Blair Atholl on a southbound train, but nonetheless showing Smith's buffer beam lettering style.

[Ellis collection 35746

Plate 18. 'Small Ben' Class 4-4-0 No. 14 *Ben Dearg* in sparkling condition at Kyle of Lochalsh showing Smith's cab-side and smokebox number and tender lettering styles.   Note the oval works plate, being that of Lochgorm.   *[Real Photographs 44801*

water capacity and extended the coal rails towards the rear of some Jones and Drummond tenders; experimented with superheaters and feed-water heaters; and designed and had built the splendid 'River' Class 4-6-0s which the HR Civil Engineer refused to accept, resulting in their sale to the Caledonian Railway and Smith's enforced resignation.   The passage of time has shown this action to have been rather unjustified, the new LMS Railway returning the 'Rivers' to the Highland Section where they worked until World War II.

However, the story has been told elsewhere, so we will not dwell further on this fascinating episode.

Smith's changes in HR locomotive livery were said to have been brought about by the conditions of World War I, commencing as they did in August 1914.   An immediate prohibition on the use of strategic materials led to a brass shortage.   To keep the Lochgorm brass foundry going, cab side number plates were removed, melted down and used for essential valves, steam fittings and so on.   In their place, locomotive running numbers were painted on, high up on the cab sides - Plate 18.

Perversely in view of the foregoing, on a few engines, the painted numerals on front buffer beams were deleted and replaced by small alloy numerals

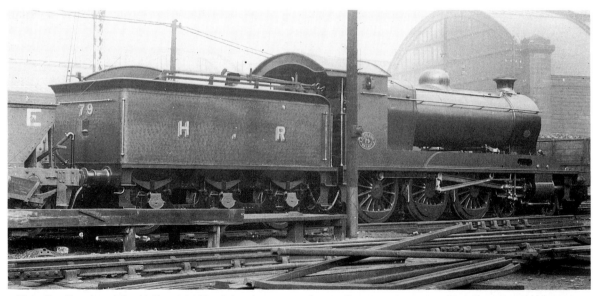

Plate 19. 'Superheated Goods' Class 4-6-0 No. 79 brand new at Hawthorn Leslie, Newcastle on 8th October 1919, showing Cumming's livery, with gunmetal style of number plate.   *[LCGB Ken Nunn collection - 2390*

Plate 20. 'Superheated Goods' Class No. 80 brand new and with the motion still to be fitted at Hawthorn Leslie, Newcastle on 8th October 1919, showing Cumming's buffer beam lettering.
[LCGB Ken Nunn collection - 2392

fitted to the top of the smokebox door. These numerals were of elaborate design, being of the scroll style (e.g. "7" was as an inverted "2", notably that on No. 70 *River Ness*). Not only that, but they were labour-intensive to fabricate, requiring much effort in cutting out, filing and fitting each number. See Plate 18.

Vermilion buffer beams reappeared, lettered " H (hook) R " only. See Plate 17.

A subtle change in the " H · R " tender and tank legend was to place the full stop on the horizontal centre line of the initials - Plate 18. However, at

least one engine, 'New Ben' 4-4-0 No. 60 *Ben Bhreac Mhor*, received the Smith treatment on the engine but the legend **HIGHLAND RAILWAY** on its own, original 3600-gallon tender.

Smith's livery was not applied consistently, hybrid liveries resulting. One such was recorded in 1915 on No. 119 *Loch Insh* which received the buffer beam treatment but not the new numbering style, keeping Jones' cast number plates. [8]

Smith is known to have lightened the basic engine shade from dark olive green to a light moss green and also to have repainted some old goods engines with plain black boilers. However, both these styles may have owed more to economic or wartime circumstances than to aesthetic appeal, few engines being treated as described. Some of those that were, kept their painted cab-side numbers until LMS days, sometimes with a repainted and numbered buffer beam, resulting in another hybrid livery.

CHRISTOPHER CUMMING (1915-1922)

Christopher Cumming took over from Smith in October 1915, and walked straight into a crisis situation. The Highland Railway was overburdened by wartime traffic and was chronically short of engines, crews and working staff. Such was the patriotic fervour that many staff simply enlisted without informing their employers.

Of course, the Company could do little to prevent this constant drain on manpower. On the contrary, according to a register of employees in the Scottish Record Office, the Company seems to have taken quite an enlightened view: if it was believed that a man had left to enlist, he was certainly not treated the same as those who simply stopped working.

Plate 21. 'Clan' Class 4-6-0 No. 55 *Clan MacKinnon* in Cumming's livery, showing the Crest on the wheel splasher casing. The Hawthorn Leslie works plate is clearly visible quite low down on the smokebox.
[Real Photographs T6509

---

[8]   See Ken Nunn photographic collection, negatives 2010 and 2017.

Plate 22. 'Clan' Class 4-6-0 No. 49 *Clan Campbell*, showing Cumming's livery. Note the coloured coupling rod flutes. The Hawthorn Leslie works plate is just visible on the smokebox.

[HRS collection]

Plate 23. 'Loch' Class 4-4-0 No. 122 *Loch Moy* at Hawthorn Leslie, Newcastle on 18th November 1919, in exactly the same place as No. 79 but a month or so later, in Cumming's livery, showing the new gunmetal style of number plate. Note the cab detail.

[LCGB Ken Nunn collection - 2437

Often, the Company was noted as being prepared to give references or to at least consider giving the man a job after the war, rather than take the view that the man had dismissed himself and was not worthy of a reference.

Cumming was forced to borrow engines from both Scottish and English railways. For new construction, government permission was necessary and initially this was limited to existing designs: hence three more 'Castles' and three more 'Lochs' were built, albeit with slight variations from their predecessors.

Subsequently in his own classes of locomotives, for which the builders contributed much of the design and detail work as well as manufacturing them, Cumming introduced a "modern" look to the Highland with outside cylinders and piston valves, Walscheart's valve gear, superheating, Belpaire firebox, rocking grates, etc., and angular styling with casing above the running plate - see Plates 19 and 22.

Deliveries of all his own engines were badly affected by wartime material shortages, work on them often being suspended. Cast number plates reappeared on the cab sides, some of these - on the 'Superheated

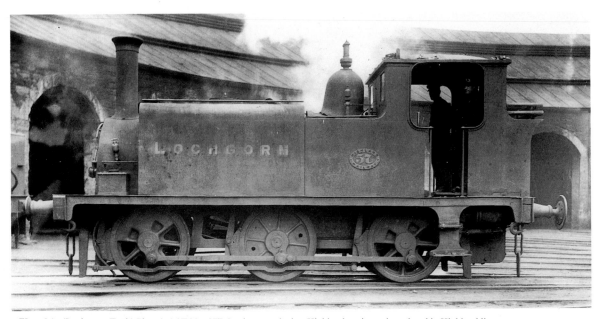

Plate 24. 'Lochgorm Tank' Class 0-6-0T No. 57B *Lochgorm* - the last Highland engine to be painted in Highland livery.

[Peter Tatlow collection

Goods' Class 4-6-0s - made of gunmetal - Plate 19 and Figure 20.

After the war, to expedite the restoration of the HR locomotive fleet, many war-weary engines were sent to English works for major overhaul. Hawthorn Leslie, Yorkshire Engine Co. and the North Eastern Railway's Gateshead and Darlington shops were the plants mainly concerned. As a result, the shades of green paint (often termed as the "nearest equivalent shade") varied considerably from the official Lochgorm moss green colour, which Cumming had deepened somewhat from the original Smith version. The engines repaired by Hawthorn Leslie were turned out, in 1920/21 at least, in a light yellowish green, which was also used on the second batch of 'Clan' Class 4-6-0s, Nos. 54 - 57, when built new by Hawthorn Leslie in 1921 - see Plates 21 and 23.

Several photographs exist of the Hawthorn Leslie repaired engines, taken before, during and after overhaul (all by CDE Roper-Nunn, brother of the better known Ken ACR Nunn). These reveal that new Cumming style number plates were cast for engines which were shown arriving with Jones and early Drummond number plates (see Plate 23), and that coupling rods were usually painted, possibly red or vermilion, after re-erection. (Note that some earlier engines on shunting duties at Inverness had had their coupling rods painted - the fact that photographs show 'Scrap Tank' No. 23 and No. 17

Needlefield so painted and otherwise spotless tends to suggest that they were smartly turned out to impress passengers.)

Cumming became seriously ill in early 1922 and resigned from office, and died shortly after.

DAVID URIE (1922)

Cumming's replacement was the son of RW Urie, CME of the London & South Western Railway. David Chalmers Urie was First Assistant to the Locomotive, Carriage & Wagon Superintendent of the Midland & Great Western Railway of Ireland - at that time, it was not good to be a British manager in Ireland. The new chief had little time left before grouping - which had already been sanctioned by Parliament - to introduce any major changes.

However, he did work out arrangements for superheating the 'New Ben' 4-4-0s. The first of these, No. 63 *Ben Mheadhoin*, appeared rebuilt in LMS days in 1923 but still in HR livery, being photographed in that condition.

Urie's only stamp on the livery was a reversion to green for buffer beams, certainly evident on HR No. 122 *Loch Moy*, the last engine to be repainted in HR colours. *Loch Moy* had previously been repainted and overhauled in 1919 by Hawthorn Leslie (Plate 23).

Plate 25. 'Big Ben' Class 4-4-0 No. 14418 *Ben Mheadhoin* neatly turned out in LMS passenger red, fully lined. Unusually, the cab doors are shut; notice that they are lined and that there is a cut-out to clear the tablet apparatus.   *[Real Photographs R6821*

Plate 26. Hawthorn Leslie displayed its first locomotive order for the Highland Railway in an unknown style of lined-out livery, fifteen years after the HR had abandoned lining out. The original print of this view reveals the works plate number as No. 3173, confirming that it was actually HR No. 74 *Durn*, masquerading as her twin sister. *[Alan Wright collection*

INTO LMS DAYS

Once the new LMS livery styles were devised and issued to paint shops, repainting in the new colours commenced, but in the meantime and well into 1923 Lochgorm continued to paint repaired engines in Highland Railway livery, some of which only involved touching up. Minor variations naturally occurred: for example, No. 70 *Loch Ashie* was noted in 1923 [9] in a Cumming-style livery but with the engine frames above the footplate painted green instead of black from the rear of the smokebox to the cab.

As a result, some late Highland repaints remained for many years afterwards, one Loch and one Castle still carrying the green in 1927 and the Inverness roundhouse shunter 0-6-0T No. 57B *Lochgorm* being the last HR engine to be repainted on overhaul in 1929 - Plate 24.

The initial post-grouping livery was, broadly, red for passenger locomotives and black for goods locomotives. Lochgorm took a generous view of the definition of passenger locomotive, and re-liveried every class in red that could possibly be justified. For example, the Banking Tanks were treated thus, on the basis that they hauled local passenger trains between Perth and Blair Atholl. Chapter 10 covers the application of LMS liveries in more detail.

There is no doubt that the Highland engines carried the red livery with aplomb. If anything, especially after years of unlined plain green, the smart lined livery can be considered with justification an improvement.

FINAL NOTES

Highland Green

As a final comment on the subject of what was or was not the "true" Highland green at any point in the periods covered by this book, it must be emphasised that the Company is on record as having purchased large quantities of "green paint" at bargain prices, shade being of a secondary consideration. The paint shop foremen at Lochgorm were then left to their own devices in the matter of "mixing and matching" to achieve the official hue. Therefore, some slight variation over a period was inevitable.

Instructions to paint shops were not necessarily laid down: even if and when they were, they were not necessarily adhered to. It has been said that the base green pigment was always the same, it was only the relative amounts of the base white, black and green that ever varied. In fact, the Yorkshire Varnish Co. supplied the HR with a bulk order for their "Quaker Green" paint in December 1901. It has also been said that the green was not green at all, but simply a mix of chrome yellow and black, their proportions varying over time. [10] We will leave the reader to

---

[9]   See Ken Nunn photographic collection, negative No. 4414, dated September 1923.
[10]   This also happened to be Sir Eric Hutchison's recipe for North British Railway gamboge.

Locomotive Livery and Insignia   25

Plate 27. This official NBL Co. broadside view of Drummond 0-6-4T No. 39 appears to show a fully lined-out and lettered locomotive ready for delivery to the Highland Railway. In reality, the three large lettering transfers bearing the company's name are still on their backing tissue which is lightly pasted to the tank side panels. The locomotive is painted in lined-out works grey for catalogue purposes, probably on one side only. It was later refinished in unlined dark olive green, with black parts, before leaving Queen's Park Works for Perth shed. *[David Jenkinson collection*

reflect, therefore, on the debate surrounding Improved Engine Green.

It is also worth noting that different degrees of discoloration, and even shedding of paint, were noticeable around the lower firebox areas of many engines after a short time in service. This is not to gainsay the excellence of maintenance of the HR loco stud (World War I crisis excepted), with paint jobs needing six weeks.

With regard to repaints carried out by outside contractors, it is likely that the firm would try to match the shade of the existing paint, with whatever they had to hand. Given that the paint would have been weathered, damaged and probably poorly maintained during World War I to boot, it is little wonder that returning locomotives would have differing hues. This comment could well be applied to new locomotives supplied during the War: *Snaigow*, *Durn* and the 1917 'Castles' and 'Lochs'.

And there is no doubt that the state of dirtiness would alter the perception of the underlying colour. Further, the state of cleanliness would likewise - the "fishscale" patterns using paraffin or oily rags demonstrate this. Finally, prevailing conditions also cause changes of colour perception: green surrounded by snow looks different from the same green surrounded by sunny summer conditions.

Regarding No. 2 Ben Alder

The well-known colour plate of HR 'Small Ben' No. 2 *Ben Alder* (on the cover of *Highland Railway Album I* by AJ Lambert, Ian Allan, 1974) depicts the engine fully lined out, but with only a single shade of green, i.e. the same shade being both inside and outside the lining panels. The spokes and balance weights of the engine wheels are shown as unlined.

It is almost certain that the painting is based on the photograph of *Ben Alder* on page 22 of the same book. Here, the locomotive is depicted in Drummond II plain livery. It can be safely concluded that in the painting the Drummond I lining has been superimposed on the Drummond II livery.

However, it has been stated that several locomotives (including 'Small Bens' Nos. 9-17) were painted in Drummond I style but using only one shade of green, being Jones apple green in order to use up existing stocks at Lochgorm. Further, even when painted in two shades of green, one was said to be a Jones apple green. [11] Despite the limited response of photographic emulsions of that era, many locomotives contemporary with *Ben Alder* were certainly photographed running in service with two shades of green, lined out in black and white (see photos of 'Small Ben' No. 10 *Ben Slioch*, 'Barney' No. 134 and 'Big Goods' No. 112 in the same book, for example), although whether one was Jones apple green cannot be substantiated.

Given the photographic shortcomings in those days, there must remain some doubt whether a single-shade livery existed in Drummond's early years, and also whether Jones apple green was used.

[11] *RCTS Highland Railway Locomotives Book I*, footnote page 11.

Regarding 'Big Goods' Nos. 103-8

Controversy surrounds the LMS 1934 restoration of HR No. 103, in respect of both its first all-green repaint and its subsequent late 1950s yellow livery.

The Yellow Debate: Notes accompanying a November 1959 SLS excursion of No. 103 from Glasgow to Blair Atholl said of the then recent repaint: "... the engine was repainted according to the original 1894 specifications which called for a change in the then standard pea green colours. The original intention was to paint all of the 4-6-0s yellow and Nos. 103/4 and possibly No. 105 appeared in this state but were speedily repainted in standard colours when it was decided that, after all, no changes should be made." See Plate 47 in the Colour Section.

It was further noted that the colour was the same as Stroudley's Improved Engine Green (also called Scotch Green). The noted historian and locomotive authority JN Maskelyne supported this, based on a photograph of No. 103 at Stanley Junction, thought to have been taken when being first delivered (see *Model Railway News* April 1960). Subsequent information modified his level of confidence, but he still concluded that on balance Nos. 103 and 104 were first painted Scotch Green (see *Model Railway News* June 1960).

Further, the equally noted authorities JRH Cormack

and JL Stevenson state in the RCTS book that "there is little doubt that ... at least up to 108 were painted yellow". However, HA Vallance and C Hamilton Ellis had the view that none were.

On balance, it would not be unreasonable to conclude that at least some 'Big Goods' appeared in service in the Stroudley yellow, even if there is disagreement on the number of engines so treated.

The Single-shade Question: A coloured plate of No. 115 in Jones livery was published in *The Railway Magazine* for July 1936, based on an original by Maurice Secretan. JN Maskelyne stated that this plate can be accepted as being correct in every detail (although there is some doubt about the shade of green). See Plate 51 in the Colour Section.

No. 103 was restored in 1934-6, being repainted in Drummond style lining and a single shade of green. The repainting would have been proposed, sanctioned and possibly executed by men who may well have themselves been in railway service when the HR 'Big Goods' were brand new in 1894. Some may have lived or even worked throughout the period these engines (and, of course, many others) were in service, witnessing all the changes of livery from Sharp Stewart's delivered finish to pre-scrapping LMS plain black. Was the 1934 repainting (certainly not a Jones style, yellow or otherwise) further evidence that a (Drummond) single shade of lined-out green did exist?

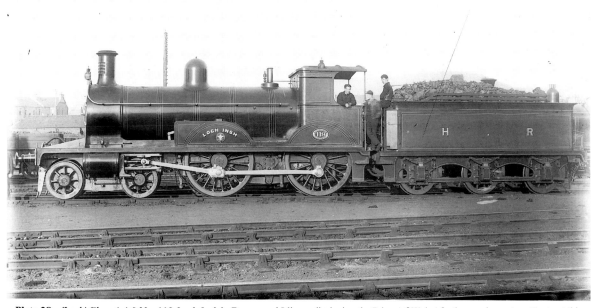

Plate 28. 'Loch' Class 4-4-0 No. 119 *Loch Insh* in Drummond I livery displaying the Prince of Wales' feathers and a garter. Contrast this with Fig. 103 in the RCTS Book I: a shot of the same locomotive in Jones' livery, taken in the same spot sometime earlier, showing the feathers in a different style without the garter but with the motto ICH DIEN. Note the latch keeping the tender-cab doors open.

[Real Photographs 14468

Regarding No. 108's works grey

A final tantalising thought is occasioned by a well-known series of photographs of No. 108 in works-grey lined-out in the Jones style with the big snowplough, taken outside Lochgorm. The locomotive having been properly liveried when delivered and only two years old when Drummond took over, there is a strong inference that the photograph was taken in Drummond's time. Hence, one might have expected any repaint to be in the Drummond I livery style, it having been delivered when new already properly painted.

Could it be that the main colour *had* been changed early on (from yellow to green)? Or that Drummond did not change the lining until after his own locomotives arrived? Or is there a more prosaic explanation, like the photographic grey being temporary for the photographs only, and simply covering the current (Jones) livery?

Regarding mis-leading photographs

Since photography itself became practicable, locomotive manufacturers have used the medium to display their products in the best possible way. Because of the limitations of early photographic emulsions, which did not easily register the favoured railway colours of green and red, it was usual to specially prepare a chosen locomotive by painting it in various shades of grey. Known as *photographic* or *works grey*, these greys were often complemented by elaborate patterns of lining out, even when the customer did not specify such embellishment, in order to further demonstrate the manufacturer's ultimate standard of finish.

Alan Wright of Newton-le-Willows, a former Hawthorn Leslie apprentice, has described how this special livery was applied, often to only one side of the locomotive, using water-based emulsions. The photographs would be taken in strictly controlled

Figure 2. A contemporary twin engraving of No. 89 *Sir George* and No. 119 *Loch Insh*, clearly showing the two-tone livery scheme and the layout of the lining. Note the positions of the near-side lamps on *Loch Insh*. The one on the buffer beam appears to be placed sideways, not in use. The other is on the rear of the tender by the tool box rather than the cab-roof as might have been expected. This twin engraving first appeared in *The Engineer* on 8th July 1898.

[*courtesy The Engineer*

lighting conditions using a large format plate camera. The negatives would be processed on site, and once the prints were made and accepted, the paint would be blasted off with a high pressure hose and the customer's specified finish applied.

Both private manufacturers and the railway company workshops occasionally resorted to catalogue painting just one locomotive of a class but lightly attaching the names and numbers of its sisters, a Hawthorn Leslie example being shown in Plate 26. This practice has recently been revived within the preservation movement to temporarily resurrect long-departed classmates of the lucky survivors.

Sometimes, locomotives and other vehicles were partially or fully painted in photographic grey so as to highlight some technical point or another. Again, after the photographic session, the paint would be simply hosed off. An example is shown in Plate 85.

Another example of works grey is a photograph of Banking Tank 0-6-4T No. 39 taken at Queen's Park Works. This shows the locomotive fully lined out. It appears that the proper company insignia have been used, namely a full transfer of "The Highland Railway." but the number plate has been painted on.

The works plate is real. See Plate 27.

A final example is that of Jones Tank 2-4-0T No. 59 *Highlander*. It has been asserted in the past that the photograph in question shows the engine in Stroudley's Improved Engine Green, but nowadays it is believed to have been shown painted in works grey, albeit with two shades of grey. See, inter alia, *RCTS Book I*, figure 55.

Quite clearly, these pictures are misleading on several counts: they show the wrong colour; the lining arrangements may be incorrect; sometimes the locomotive was given a different name and number; and sometimes the photograph itself was touched-up afterwards. Although these photographs often display an inaccurate rendering of the eventual in-service livery, they almost always reveal a wealth of mechanical detail which is invaluable to students and modellers alike.

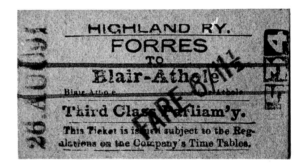

Plate 29. A study of 'Scrap Tank' Class 0-6-0T No. 22 shunting at Inverness, showing the complex Drummond company lettering style, with shading, back shading and highlights. Note the flat style of number plate and the matching Lochgorm works plate. Notice also that the coupling rods are coloured. It can just be made out that there is a lamp on each side of the cab roof, denoting that the locomotive is indeed shunting - see Chapter 9 regarding lamp positioning. *[Neil Hunter collection*

TABLE 1 - LOCOMOTIVE LIVERY

TABLE 1 LOCOMOTIVE LIVERY	JONES II 1884 - 1896	DRUMMOND I 1896 - Aug. 1902	DRUMMOND II Sept. 1902 - 1912	SMITH 1912 - 1915 [1]	CUMMING 1915 - 1922
BASIC COLOUR	Apple green	Apple green or light olive green	Dark olive green	Light moss green	Moss green [6]
SECONDARY COLOUR	Olive green	Dark olive green	None	None	None
LINING OUT	Black bands, edged with a vermilion line on olive green side and a white line on apple green side.	Black bands, edged with a white line on both sides.	None	None ('River' Class were to be "lined as required")	None
around NUMBER PLATES	Surrounded by an ellipse of lining colours		None	None	None
around WORKS PLATES			None		
SPLASHER TOPS	Olive green	Dark olive green	Dark olive green	Light moss green	Moss green
BOILER BANDS	Black bands, edged with a vermilion line on both sides; outside these on boiler proper, olive green bands edged with white lines. See Figure 3.	Black bands, edged with a white line on both sides; outside these on boiler proper, olive green bands edged with white lines. See Figure 4.	Plain	Plain	Plain
CAB ROOF	White	Black	Black	Black	Black
CAB INTERIOR (upper)	Grained	Grained	Buff	Buff	Buff
CAB INTERIOR (lower)	Olive green	Dark olive green	Dark olive green	Light moss green	Moss green
CAB SPECTACLES	Painted		Circular: Polished brass [2] Other: Painted		
CAB TO TENDER DOORS	Only 'Loch' Class so fitted in Jones' time, lined out on outside and inside faces.	Two-tone green, lined out	Dark olive green	Light moss green	Moss green
TENDER FRONT	Two-tone green, lined as panel.	Black	Black	Black	Black
TENDER TOP & COAL RAILS	Black	Black	Black	Black	Black

TABLE 1 — LOCOMOTIVE LIVERY

LOCOMOTIVE LIVERY	JONES II 1884 - 1896	DRUMMOND I 1896 - Aug 1902	DRUMMOND II Sept. 1902 - 1912	SMITH 1912 - 1915 [1]	CUMMING 1915 - 1922
SMOKEBOX	Black	Black	Black	Black	Black
CHIMNEY	Black with polished copper over the wider lip of the cap.	Black	Black	Black	Black
SAFETY VALVES	Polished brass	Polished brass	Polished brass	Polished brass	Polished brass
WHISTLE	Polished brass	Polished brass	Polished brass	Polished brass	Polished brass
HANDRAILS	Polished	Polished	Polished	Polished	Polished
VISIBLE PIPEWORK:					
BOILER FEEDS & CLACKS	Polished	Polished	Polished	Polished	Polished
INJECTOR FEEDS & VALVES	Not common externally; Nos. 101/2 polished	Polished	Polished	Polished	Polished
EJECTOR EXHAUST	Not common externally, '101' Class only painted.	Not common externally, '101' Class only painted.	Painted	Painted	Painted as background
STEAMCHEST LUBRICATORS	Polished	Polished	Polished	Polished	Polished
OILBOXES [3]	Polished	Polished	Polished	Polished	Polished
REVERSING RODS (visible)	Polished	Polished	Polished	Polished	Painted / polished ends
SANDBOX LINING	Sandboxes which were integral with the adjacent splashers were lined out to follow the internal shape of the box, and separated from the splasher lining. Note especially the 'Castle' Class.	None	None	None	None
FOOTPLATE TOPS	Black	Black	Black	Black	Black
FOOTPLATE VALANCES	Claret, edged with black bands, separated with vermilion lines, with yellow line along bottom edge.	Claret, edged with black bands, separated with white lines, with yellow line along bottom edge. Sometimes, top band/line omitted, no yellow line.	Dark olive green	Light moss green	Moss green
FOOTPLATE STEPS	Claret, lined as valances, with black treads.	Claret, lined as valances, with black treads.	Dark olive green / black	Light moss green / black	Moss green / black

TABLE 1 LOCOMOTIVE LIVERY	JONES II 1884 - 1896	DRUMMOND I 1896 - Aug. 1902	DRUMMOND II Sept. 1902 - 1912	SMITH 1912 - 1915 [1]	CUMMING 1915 - 1922
BUFFER BEAMS	Claret, with vermilion panel, edged with a white line, then black band, then red line. [4]	Claret, with vermilion panel, lined yellow / black / yellow. [4]	Dark olive green	Vermilion	Vermilion
BUFFER SHANKS	Claret, lined black / yellow / red at front lip.	Claret, lined yellow / black / yellow midway along shank.	Dark olive green	Light moss green	Moss green
ENGINE FRAMES:					
CREWE-TYPE	Claret, edged with black band; inside a red line, outside a yellow line.	Claret, edged with black band; inside a red line, outside a yellow line.	Dark olive green	Light moss green	Moss green
NORMAL - above footplate	Claret, edged with black band; inside a red line, outside a yellow line.	Varied: claret, green or black	Dark olive green	Black ('Rivers' to be "green")	Black
NORMAL - below footplate	Black, except bogie frame fronts: claret, lined out.	Black	Black	Black ('Rivers' to be "green")	Black
INSIDE FACES	Vermilion	Black	Black	Vermilion ('Rivers' to be "black")	Vermilion
TENDER FRAMES:					
1800 GALLON	Claret, lined as for Crewe-type engine frames.	Claret, lined as for Crewe-type engine frames.	Dark olive green	Light moss green	Moss green
NORMAL	Claret, lined as for Crewe-type engine frames, but horns and springs black.	Claret, lined as for Crewe-type engine frames, but horns claret and springs black.	Black	Black	Black, some moss green later.
8-WHEEL	None in Jones time.	Black	Black	Black	Black
INSIDE FACES	Black	Black	Black	Black	Black
GUARD IRONS - front & rear	Vermilion on engines, none on Jones tenders.	Black, but some tipped vermilion at front end.	Black, but some tipped vermilion at front end	Vermilion front, black on tender.	Vermilion front, black on tender.

TABLE 1 LOCOMOTIVE LIVERY	JONES II 1884 - 1896	DRUMMOND I 1896 - Aug. 1902	DRUMMOND II Sept. 1902 - 1912	SMITH 1912 - 1915[1]	CUMMING 1915 - 1922
ENGINE WHEEL CENTRES	Apple green, with white lines around bosses and along each spoke, forked at each spoke end. Olive green segments within inner forks.	Apple green, with white lines around bosses and along each spoke, forked at each spoke end. Olive green segments within inner forks.	Dark olive green	Light moss green	Moss green
BALANCE WEIGHTS	Olive green, lined vermilion/black/white.	Dark olive green, lined black / white.	Dark olive green	Light moss green	Moss green
AXLE ENDS (Visible)	Olive green, circled vermilion/black/white.	Dark olive green, circled white.	Dark olive green	Light moss green	Black
TENDER WHEEL CENTRES	Apple green, unlined except on older tenders.	6-wheel as for Jones; 8-wheel lined.	Dark olive green	Light moss green	Moss green
ALL TYRES	Black	Black	Black	Black	Black
AXLE SHAFTS	Vermilion	Black	Black	Vermilion	Vermilion
OUTSIDE CYLINDERS:					
CREWE-TYPE	Black, with green panel lined white line / black band / vermilion line.	Black, with green panel lined white line / black band / white line.	Black	Black	Black
NORMAL	Black, with large Apple green panel lined white line / black band / vermilion line.[5]	'Castles': black, with claret panel lined white line / black band / white line. Others: black, with green panel.[5]	Dark olive green	Light moss green	Moss green
END COVERS	Crewe-type engines: white or polished. It is said that enginemen kept a tin of whitewash on the footplate, to spruce up the covers at the end of every journey. Others: black.			Crewe-type engines: white or polished. Polishing often abandoned, the covers being painted instead, presumably due to WWI shortage of labour. Others: black.	
RODS & VALVE GEAR	Polished	Plain steel	Plain steel, but some painted (red?)	Polished	Polished, with some fluting: vermilion.

TABLE 1 — LOCOMOTIVE LIVERY

FITTINGS:	JONES II 1884 - 1896	DRUMMOND I 1896 - Aug. 1902	DRUMMOND II Sept. 1902 - 1912	SMITH 1912 - 1915 [1]	CUMMING 1915 - 1922
SMALL brass FITTINGS	Usually polished	-	-	-	-
BRAKE COLUMNS & HOSES	Black	Black	Black	Black	Black
COUPLING LINKS & HOOKS	Polished	Polished	Polished	Plain in WWI	Polished after WWI
WESTINGHOUSE PUMPS	Pump Cylinder Jackets painted in the boiler colour, and, if locomotive lined, also lined round their top and bottom edges.				
SNOWPLOUGH ANGLE IRONS	Not fitted. Ploughs bolted to guard irons.	Usually removed from engines if no snow.		Vermilion in situ	Vermilion in situ
SNOWPLOUGH	Claret wooden parts, black ironwork, varnished				
LAMPS	Body: signal red. Bulls-eye: red, green or white when lit, clear when unlit.				
WARNING BOARDS [7]	Signal red with white letters, shaded black to lower right.				
TABLET CATCHER	None [8]	Jaws bright steel, rest black.			
PASSENGER ALARM BELL [9]	Gong: polished - probably brass. Mechanism: painted either green or black	None [10]		None	None

[1] Very few engines carried the Smith livery.

[2] Drummond-designed engines only.

[3] On many tender axleboxes; also on leading axleboxes of 2-4-0s; and those above the leading splashers of Jones 4-4-0 Classes.

[4] Crewe-type locomotives were lined on outside edges also.

[5] 'Big Goods', 'Loch' and 'Yankee Tank (101)' Classes.

[6] Except for Nos. 54-57, which were yellowish green instead of moss green, throughout.

[7] ENGINE FOLLOWING red board at the front and UP/DOWN red disk at the rear of the train. Possibly also LAST Board. See Chapter 9 - Lamp Codes for further details.

[8] Introduced on the Highland from 1899 on.

[9] Drummond locomotives are believed not to have had an alarm bell apparatus. Instead, early Drummond locomotives had a folding arm on the right-hand tender coping and a groove and channel on the engine cab-roofs so that the passenger alarm cord formerly connected to the tender gong on Jones' engines could be used to sound the Drummond engine whistle. These features are shown on the Drummond drawings, but no photos of the whistle and cord so connected have come to light.

[10] Progressively removed from 1903 as the passenger coach alarm cord system was replaced by a chain (i.e. the communication cord) connected to the vacuum brake.

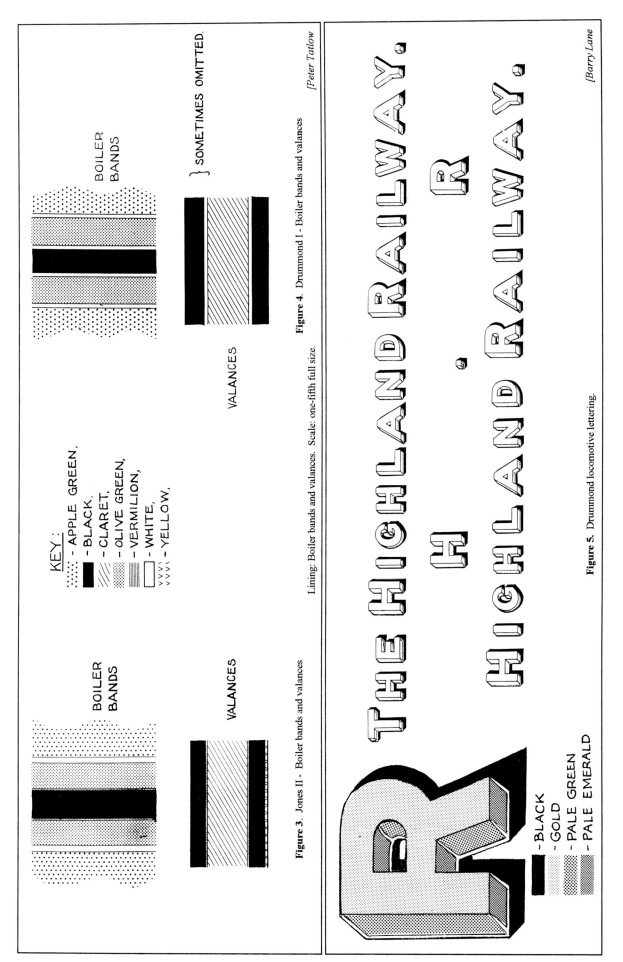

KEY:
:::::::: - APPLE GREEN,
███ - BLACK,
////// - CLARET,
░░░░ - OLIVE GREEN,
≡≡≡ - VERMILION,
□ - WHITE,
ⱱⱱⱱⱱ - YELLOW,

BOILER BANDS

VALANCES

Figure 3. Jones II - Boiler bands and valances

BOILER BANDS

VALANCES

} SOMETIMES OMITTED.

[Peter Tatlow]

Lining: Boiler bands and valances. Scale: one-fifth full size.

Figure 4. Drummond I - Boiler bands and valances

THE HIGHLAND RAILWAY.
H
HIGHLAND RAILWAY.

[Barry Lane]

███ - BLACK
░░░ - GOLD
▒▒▒ - PALE GREEN
▓▓▓ - PALE EMERALD

Figure 5. Drummond locomotive lettering.

TABLE 2 - LOCOMOTIVE INSIGNIA

TABLE 2 LOCOMOTIVE INSIGNIA	JONES II 1884 - 1896	DRUMMOND I 1896 - 1905	DRUMMOND II 1905 - 1912	SMITH 1912 - 1915	CUMMING 1915 - 1922
ENGINE NUMBER PLATES:			See also Chapter 7.		
STYLE	Elliptical brass with letters of company name sunken around rim and infilled black.	Elliptical brass with block letters of company name sunken around rim and infilled black.	Elliptical, double rim enclosing company name, polished.	Removed due to brass famine in WWI.	Elliptical, double rim enclosing company name, polished. Some made of gun metal.
NUMERALS	Scroll-style, raised and polished against a vermilion background.	Sunken in plate and infilled black.	Block-style, raised and polished.	Numbers painted high on cab-side.	Block-style, raised and polished. Nos. 73 and 74 had scroll-style numerals and serifed letters.
SIZE	Nominal 17" x 11.25"	17" x 11.25"	22.5" x 15"	-	22.5" x 15"
WORKS PLATES	Varied according to makers: see Chapter 8.				
HR CREST / GARTER	Not used	Not used	Not used	Not used	10" diameter [1]
LETTERING STYLE	Gold block letters: See Frontispiece and Plate 29.	Shaded left very light green; below darker green. High-lighted white on sides, bottoms and transitions; outlined in thin black lines. Counter-shaded right and below in black.	See also Figure 5.	Some consider shading all one green. White highlights along the bottom edge do not appear to have been universal; they may have become more prevalent during Cummings time.	
LETTERING SIZES:					
H . R	Not used	9" x 7"	9" x 7"	9" x 7"	12" x 7.5" [2]
THE HIGHLAND RAILWAY.	Not used	Initials (T H R) 9" x 7" Others 7" x 7"		Discontinued WWI	Not used (H . R only on repaint)
HIGHLAND RAILWAY.	Not used	Initials (H R) 9" x 7" Others 7" x 7"		Discontinued WWI	Not used (H . R only on repaint)
ENGINE NAMES [3]	4" high. Some initial letters 6" or 7" high.	4" high. Some initial letters 6" or 7" high.	All 4" high.	All 4" high.	All 4" high.
BUFFER BEAM CHARACTERS	Not used	9" x 7"		9" x 7"	9" x 7"

TABLE 2 — LOCOMOTIVE INSIGNIA

LOCOMOTIVE INSIGNIA	JONES II 1884 - 1896	DRUMMOND I 1896 - 1905	DRUMMOND II 1905 - 1912	SMITH 1912 - 1915	CUMMING 1915 - 1922
BUFFER BEAM APPLICATIONS	Not used	"H . R (hook) NNN" Bens 1-9: "H . R (hook) No. N" (the "o" is underscored)	"H . R (hook) NNN"	"H (hook) R" only [4]	"No. (hook) NNN" (the ' o" is underscored)
REAR NOs. (Bunkers and Tenders)	4.5" high on tender rear coping. [5]	9" high		9" high	9" high

EMBELLISHMENTS

Crews applied special finishes to their locomotives at all periods. Examples are:
Paint removed from outer edges of smokebox, wingplates and cylinders, etc. and burnished.
Stars, leaves, thistle emblems and masons symbols (hammer and trowel) applied to smokebox doors.

The Prince of Wales feathers, with and without garter surround, worn by No. 119 *Loch Insh* was a one-off official embellishment, for a September 1896 royal duty taking the Duke of York from Perth to Grantown-on-Spey (one of the last duties undertaken by David Jones). Photographed with feathers without garter in Jones livery, and with (different) feathers and garter in Drummond I livery - Plate 28.

[1] The Crest was the Garter "filled" with the Coat of Arms. The Garter on its own was "empty". See page 49 for illustration and heraldic description. Applied when new to Nos. 73,74, 'Clans', 1917 'Castles', and to a few earlier 'Castles' upon repaint after WWI (e.g. Crest on No. 142 *Dunrobin Castle*).
Application: Nos. 73,74: on centre of the leading splashers, below the name. Garter only when new; eventually Crest.
'Clan' Class: on the narrower, rear section of the splasher casings.
1917 'Castles': on the centre sandboxes.

[2] The full stop was often on the horizontal centre-line of the H and R, as in "**H · R**"

[3] Engine names were applied inside the curve of the leading splashers of 4-coupled tender engines and with one word on each of the leading and centre splashers of the 'Castle' Class 4-6-0s, the names being inside the lining on the light green shade during the lined periods.
On the 'Clan' Class 4-6-0s, the names were applied in a straight line along the subsidiary splasher casings, the centre letter being near to the dome centre line.
Tank engine names were applied in a straight line along the side tanks. In Jones' time, small tank engines, if named, used 7" and 9" letters. In later periods, if the full title was applied, 4" letters were used.
It is worth noting that the original 2-4-0T No. 59 *Highlander*, as shown in workshop photographic livery, has its letters shaded to the right hand side.

[4] Some engines ran in hybrid style with "H (hook) R" on buffer beam, and also cab number plates, probably WWI touch-ups.

[5] There is some doubt about this, although on balance it is probably so, at least latterly. See 'Skye Bogie' Class No. 88 at Helmsdale and 'Big Goods' Class No. 113 at Stanley in *Highland Railway Album* pp 13 and 17 respectively, where their numbers are believed discernible, very small on top lip of tank rear.

Plate 30. Embellishments 1 - 'Clan' Class 4-6-0 No. 54 *Clan Chattan* on a local train showing thistle and star-burst decorations on the smokebox door.
[HL Salmon collection 1339 - courtesy The Stephenson Locomotive Society

Plate 31. Embellishments 2 - 'Castle' Class 4-6-0 No. 144 *Blair Castle* all dolled up at Inverness in June 1906. Peter Drummond himself is on the right. When No. 141 *Ballindalloch Castle* was similarly decorated for heading the Royal Train, it is apparent that the same stag's head was used. However, the reigning monarch had far less undergrowth and leafery than festooned No. 144. *[L&GRP 12428*

CHAPTER 2 - COACHING STOCK LIVERY AND INSIGNIA

This Chapter covers all passenger coaches, including full brake and luggage vans, Pullmans, sleeping and dining cars, and other vehicles which carried, as their prime purpose, passengers and/or their luggage. Post Office vans are also included.

COACH GREEN

From 1874 onwards the standard coaching stock green was the same as on locomotives, the darker shade being used during the time when locomotives were painted in a two-colour style.

TWO-TONE LIVERY

In 1896 the Duke of Sutherland took delivery of a private saloon carriage designed for him by David Jones. The livery consisted of dark olive green with the upper sunken panels picked out in white. The appearance of this vehicle on their system so impressed the Highland's Board of Directors that Jones was instructed to apply the scheme to the Directors' own saloon, together with two HR family saloons and a 4-wheeled passenger brake van.

This work was actually completed after Peter Drummond took over. After inspecting the finished vehicles, the Board gave orders to apply the two-tone livery to all passenger vehicles and brake/luggage vans. The new scheme soon appeared on main line stock and then spread gradually to most other coaches until, from August 1902, economic considerations forced the HR to discontinue the white upper panels and revert to an all-green livery. However, the Directors' Saloon remained two-tone until 1924 or so.

In all probability, some of the older and smaller coaches never received the white upper panels, while it is just possible that some coaches painted in the two colours up to 1902 ran in this condition until the start of WWI.

On panelled coaches, the white colour was applied to the sunken panel surface above the waist together with the bolections, all raised mouldings and droplight frames being finished in green. All side panels were lined gold or yellow. See Plates 32, 33 and 34.

Ribbed sided coaches, which of course had no panels, were not excluded from the application of the new two-tone livery, as is evidenced in the RCTS *HR Locomotives Book 1* in Figure 77 on page 112.

Plate 32. Built circa 1888, Jones' D21 Third-class Saloon No. 53 in Drummond's two-tone livery. Note the label board, the very widely spaced 'H . R', and the communication cord along the eaves. *[Ellis collection 12319*

VARNISH AND PULLMAN LIVERIES

Sleeping Carriages Nos. 8 and 9, and Third Class Excursion Saloons Nos. 195 and 196, all built by contractors in 1906, were of matchboard exterior construction and were finished in highly varnished natural teak. These four vehicles retained this finish for some 10 years, until repainted green in WWI. No other Highland coaches were so treated. See Plate 35. The Pullman Cars which operated over the Highland system at certain times ran in their standard dark brown livery with gold lining and lettering, although "standard" certainly did not mean "plain" - see Plate 98.

INSIGNIA

The insignia carried by coaches varied over the years, as well as between stock of the same age.

Up to 1897:

Passenger carriages displayed a plain **garter**, which had a gold rim surrounding the vehicle number. The company name was in the rim. The garter was placed near the middle of each coach side. In addition, a **monogram** was placed towards each end of the coach. This comprised the initials HR in an elaborate script lettering, an example of which is shown in Plate 36. A similar yet noticeably different representation exists in a drawing of a chariot ended carriage, as shown below.

A similar style is shown on the Station Master's cap in *Highland Railway Album*.

The **class designation** was given in full on all coaches of uniform class:

FIRST CLASS or **THIRD CLASS**

whereas on composite coaches the words

FIRST or **SECOND** or **THIRD**

appeared on each compartment door at waist level. All **lettering** was in gold, serifed letters, although block letters may have appeared just before Jones' departure. At least sometimes, the first letter, certainly the F and perhaps the T and C, was slightly larger than the rest:

FIRST CLASS or **THIRD CLASS**

These differing sizes applied to all periods. See Plates 38 and 36.

1897 - c.1907:

After 1897, the **monogram**s were deleted and the **lettering** changed to gold block (similar to below), shaded as for locomotive lettering:

FIRST CLASS or **THIRD CLASS**

The **initials** H.R were applied once to each side, usually offset to the left of middle and at waist level.

Plate 33. Drummond's 1902-built D38 6-wheel Passenger Brake Van No. 67, showing the two-tone livery to advantage. (The chimney-like construction above the roof is in fact a signal-wire post in the background.) *[Ellis collection 4589*

The amount of offset was dependent upon whatever was convenient given the panelling. The spacing of the initials varied widely, sometimes being two or three feet apart. On guards' compartments, however, they were usually on the lookouts, without the full stop and higher up.

The vehicle **number** on the longer coaches appeared twice each side towards each end. On shorter coaches, the number appeared once, offset to the right of middle, symmetrically with the initials; the number spacing did not vary. As with the initials, the number was usually on the lookout of the guard's compartment, but still at waist level. However, bogie brake vans of 1904 (Diagram 64) had numbers twice on each side towards the ends, as on coaches, and *not* on lookouts.

The **garter** now appeared twice each side towards each end, although probably not on brake vans and the like. Plate 39 shows a typical example of this livery style.

Passenger brake vans had legends for **GUARD** (on the guard's door) and **LUGGAGE VAN** (on waist panels) - see Plate 33.

c.1907 - 1912:

Applied first to Diagram 54 bogie composites built in 1907, the **initials** and **numbers** were enlarged to 9" and placed just below waist level. Often, the letters were smaller than the numbers. Their vertical alignment vis-à-vis the larger numbers could be to the top, to the bottom, or midway. Around 1910, the **class designations** also moved down, sometimes as far as to align along the lower edge of all insignia, sometimes still very high. **Garters** and Guard / Luggage Van legends were still applied. Each of the few surviving photographs seem to show a slightly different configuration! Plate 40 shows an example.

Drummond 3rd class 6-wheel coaches to Diagram 22 apparently had the **class designations** on their sides but not on the doors, although the only known photographs show them on the door as usual. See Plate 41.

The company initials and number were applied to corridor gangway shutters, one under the other and in white. They were initially about 4" high, increasing to 9" latterly. See Plate 43.

After 1912:

After 1912, the vehicle **numbers** were made larger still, now being applied once only left of and near the middle on 6-wheel vehicles and twice near the ends on bogie coaches. **Letters** followed suit, appearing right of middle or middle respectively.

These last alterations coincided with the general introduction of matchboard siding for new coaches. Panelled coaches were sometimes, but not always, repaired with matchboard siding; panelled coaches lasted well into the LMS period.

From the end of 1912, the full **crest** took the place of the garter, appearing twice on each side, though the garter was retained on older coaches when they were repainted in all-green livery. The **garter** was also etched into the frosted glass of the lavatory windows in Drummond's coaches (see Plate 35), but disappeared altogether on the older 4-wheeled coaches. Another form of etched lavatory window is shown in Plate 42. Passenger brake vans continued

Plate 34. Drummond's 1898-built D16 Type H bogie Composite/Lav No. 47, showing the two-tone livery to advantage. This coach was one of two that were the first in the family of standard bogie composites, and were first allocated to the Inverness and Edinburgh through service: note the label board "INVERNESS FORTH BRIDGE & DUNKELD". *[AJ Lambert collection*

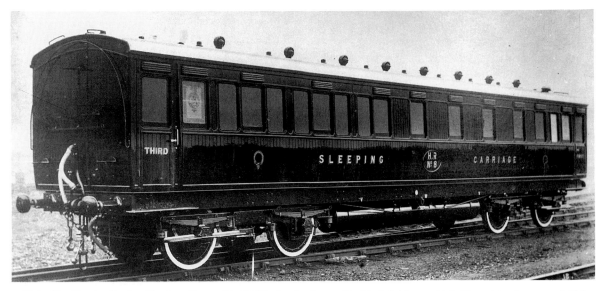

Plate 35. Sleeping Carriage No. 8 to Diagram 53 of 1906, showing the varnished teak finish, moulded ellipse style of company initials and number, and the lavatory window with etched crest.

[HMRS collection T16/41

Plate 36. Jones coach monogram and First Class designation (block style). This is an enlarged fragment of a rare photograph, and is not of the highest quality, but it is the only known example of the monogram. Compare with the drawing on page 40.

[Peter Tatlow collection

Plate 37. Jones Third Class designation on the inside of a door (block style). *[Mark Tatlow*

Plate 38. Jones Third Class designation (block style), from grounded coach at Boat Of Garten. *[Peter Tatlow*

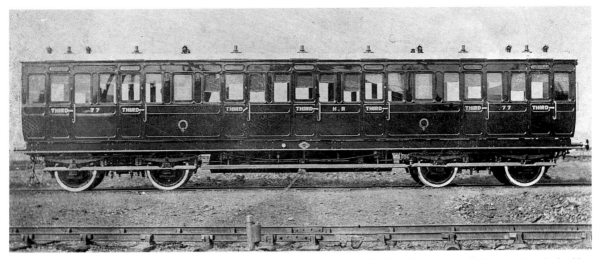

Plate 39. Third Class No. 77 of 1903 to Diagram 29, showing the Drummond style of small insignia at waist level and two body-side garters. *[HMRS collection W414*

to have the legends for **GUARD** (on the single door) and **LUGGAGE VAN** (on waist panels).

Sleeping and Excursion Saloons:

The 1906 series of Sleeping and Excursion Saloons had a **moulded ellipse** on the middle of each side carrying the company initials and vehicle number - see Plate 35.

Post Office Vans:

Post Office Vans were not numbered before 1899 - as evidenced in the HR's Traffic Committee Minutes for 31st January 1899.

LABEL BOARDS

The destination of or the route taken by carriages were displayed either by temporary paper labels placed on quarter-lights or by permanent label boards, of which there were two types. The first was a small board which was slipped in place on the carriage side above a quarter light, stating the destination station, e.g. Ballinluig, or the route as in Plates 32 and 34. Often, the board was lettered on both sides, e.g. Ballinluig and Aberfeldy. The second was a much larger affair altogether, again slipped into locators but on the coach roof. One quoted example, for sleepers running between Glasgow and Inverness, is: "The Highland Railway. The Royal Route, Glasgow Buchanan Street and Inverness via Dunkeld." Others were more succinct.

The scarcity of photographs is perhaps surprising, since these boards contained most important information. One of the authors has a sketch by Alice Liddell (the *real* Alice in Wonderland) *"With our parcels we make a start from Inverness"* (for Skye). There are crude outlines of two carriages, yet she has observed on the roofs the label boards marked Inverness and Dingwall respectively.

Plate 40. Brake Lavatory Corridor Composite No. 18 of 1911 to Diagram 57, showing Drummond's large style insignia. Note the different sizes of the letters and numbers, with class designations vertically aligned to the top; and the hybrid style with the letters and numbers repeated on the guard's lookout. *[HRS collection*

Plate 41. Third Class No. 140 of 1909 to Diagram 22, showing another version of the large insignia. Note the class designations do not align with the letters and numbers. *[Ellis collection* 13947

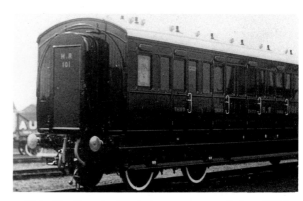

Plate 43. Example of insignia on a gangway shutter. Third Class No. 101 of 1909 to Diagram 60.

[David Jenkinson collection

Plate 42 - above. Etched lavatory window in a thistle motif - from Jones' chariot 6-wheel 1st. Contrast with that of the coach depicted in Plate 35. *[Duncan Wheeler*

Plate 44. Break-down between Brora and Loth, May 1914. No. 80 is a Type L all third Pickering coach built 1903 to Diagram 29. These were semi-corridor with lavatories accessible from only four of the seven compartments. *[David Jenkinson collection*

Plate 45. Smoking compartment designation from Jones' chariot 6-wheel 1st. *[Duncan Wheeler*

CARRIAGE SHEETS

Up till now, there seems to have been no awareness that these objects even existed. The possibility was first mooted when the author studied a photograph enlarged for other reasons. [12]

John Roake recently pointed out Rule 167, 1888 Rule Book, which confirms the existence of Carriage Sheets, albeit obliquely:

> "At Stations where Passenger Plant is kept, the Station Agents are to see the vehicles are always in good order, the windows kept closed, and the ventilators open; that they are always kept under cover, where accommodation is afforded for that purpose, and, where there is no Carriage-shed, that they are covered with sheets to protect them from the sun."

There are but two known photographs, [13] both of the same subject, which show what these Sheets looked like. Study of much enlarged portions shows a siding at Blair Athole with a train of nine four-wheel rib-sided carriages by the north-bound platform, plus what seem to be two spares at the buffers. All but one have roof lamps in place. Of these, eight have their sides and at least one end if not both sheeted, and the roofs left uncovered.

As far as can be made out, the only unsheeted carriages are two all-thirds and the brake van, all the first or composite class carriages being sheeted. It cannot be determined whether this is significant or not! Perhaps Blair Athole only had an allocation of eight sheets.

Of several sheets that can be read to varying degrees under the magnifying glass, at least two are on upside down.

They appear to be attached by hooking the edges of the sheet over the external communication cord eyes, situated along the top of the sides. The fixing has not been executed particularly neatly, the sheets taking on a rather undulating appearance. The sheets are identified to the station and are numbered: at Blair Athole, numbers 1, 2 and probably 3 can all be made out. Some are marked as below; some have a fuller **"HIGHLAND RY."** marking.

The sheets' total size can only be guessed: at around 30 feet per side, they might have been anything up to 76 feet long by 8 feet high. They look white in colour (one looks quite dirty), no doubt to reflect the sun. The colour of the block lettering is unknown, but certainly dark - we might suppose chocolate brown. They are presumably rain-proof, and hence likely to be made of tarpaulin.

They must have been quite unwieldy to handle. Arrangements for storage and deployment are not known.

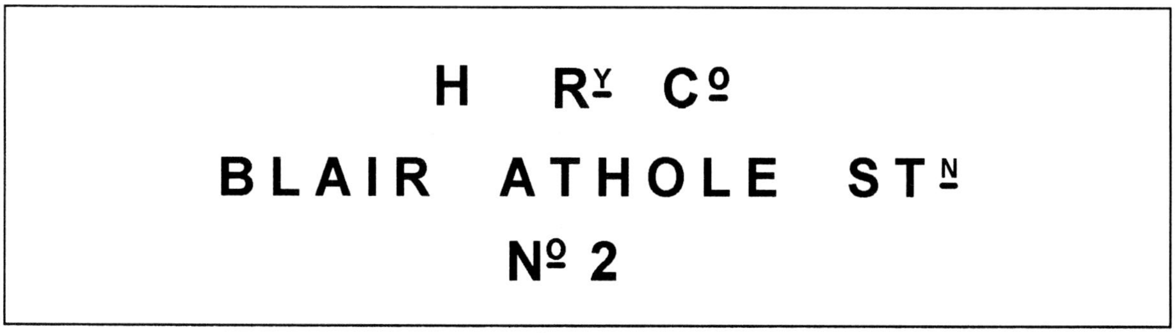

H R$^{\underline{Y}}$ C$^{\underline{O}}$

BLAIR ATHOLE ST$^{\underline{N}}$

N$^{\underline{O}}$ 2

Figure 6. Example of the layout of lettering on one side of a carriage sheet. Not to scale. *[Howard Geddes*

---

[12]   The enlargement (of a George Washington Wilson plate B486X, showing Blair Athole station) was published in *Highland Railway Journal No. 27 (Autumn 1993)*. The date is unknown, but was probably the early 1880s.

[13]   The other being B487, taken at same time.

TABLE 3 – CARRIAGE LIVERY

TABLE 3 CARRIAGE LIVERY	JONES II 1884 - 1896	DRUMMOND I 1896 - Aug. 1902	DRUMMOND II Sept. 1902 - 1912	SMITH 1912 - 1915	CUMMING 1915 - 1922
MAIN BODY COLOUR	Dark olive green	Dark olive green	Dark olive green	Light moss green	Moss green
SECONDARY COLOUR	None	White uppers	None	None	None
LINING	Gold or yellow on edge of mouldings, by panels.	Gold or yellow on edge of mouldings, by panels.	None	None	None
ROOF (ex-works)	White	White	Medium grey (Nos. 195/196: white)	White	White
COMPARTMENT LAMP TOPS & VENTS	White	White	Black	White	White
ENDS (all stock except as below)	Dark olive green	Dark olive green	Dark olive green	Light moss green	Moss green
ENDS (Post Office vans and 4 & 6 wheel brake/guards vans)		Bright red (vermilion?). Possibly green once bogie coaches were in use. [1]			
BUFFER SHANKS		Same as the Ends			
END STEPS & RAILS		Black			
VESTIBULE CONNECTIONS	None	None	Black, with white letters and number, e.g. **H R 101** 4" then 9" high.	Black	Black
EXTERNAL LAMPS			Signal red		
UNDERFRAMES, BOGIES, etc.			Black		
WHEEL CENTRES		Mansell wheels almost universal with varnished segments (teak) and black iron braces and bolt heads etc., when new.			
TYRES (ex-works)			White		
PULLMAN CARS [2]	Pullman Co. colours: brown livery with gold lettering etc.			Not used by HR	As before, except now brown and cream.

[1] Probably discontinued for the same economic reasons as white upper panels from August 1902, but those vehicles on branch line sets would carry them for years after.

[2] Used on Perth-Inverness services only, 1885-1907. In 1922, the Caledonian Railway ran one to Aviemore only.

TABLE 4 – CARRIAGE INSIGNIA

TABLE 4 CARRIAGE INSIGNIA	JONES II 1884 – 1896	DRUMMOND I 1896 – 1904	DRUMMOND II 1904 – 1912	SMITH 1912 – 1915	CUMMING 1915 – 1922
INSIGNIA STYLE	Gold serifed until 1894, then block.	Gold block shaded, same as locomotive style.	Gold block shaded, same as locomotive style.	Gold block shaded, same as locomotive style.	Gold block shaded, same as locomotive style.
INSIGNIA SIZES:					
CLASS — SIZE	Approx. 4" high. First letter(s). e.g. F. T. C. sometimes somewhat bigger, say 5" (see Plates 36 and 38).				
CLASS — POSITION	On waist panels of Jones and Drummond stock (see Plates 32 and 39). Below waistline to varying degrees on matchboard stock (e.g. see Plate 41).				
COMPANY INITIALS — SIZE	Monogram style, gold script, approx. 9" x 15"	Approx. 4" or 7" high, then 9" and latterly probably 12".			
COMPANY INITIALS — POSITION	Towards each end.	H.R once each side.			spacing of H and R varied.
NUMBERS — SIZE	Approx. 4" high (?)	Approx. 4" or 7" high, then 9" and latterly probably 12".			
NUMBERS — POSITION	Not known, possibly on waist panels.	Short coaches: once right of middle, symmetrically with H.R. Long coaches: twice towards each end.	Offset left of middle if one number per side. In middle if two numbers per side.		
LETTERING e.g. Guard, Luggage Van. — SIZE	Not known.	Same as Class; some lettering (e.g. SLEEPING CARRIAGE) same as HR initials or numbers.			
LETTERING — POSITION	Not known.	GUARD on door, others variable: waist level or body side symmetrically (see Plates 35 and 40).			
HR GARTER	Gold, nominal diameter 10"	Same as in Jones' time, also etched into lavatory windows by Drummond (see Plate 35). Garter retained on older types of coach until 1922.			
HR CREST	None	None			New vestibule coaches only: twice each side.
EXTERNAL INFORMATION, etc.					
HOME STATION NAME	Branch coaches painted with home station name in 3" white letters on vehicle solebars.				
SMOKING LABELS	SMOKING etched on quarter light glass, three-quarters of the way up (see Plate 45).				
LABEL BOARDS	Label Boards fixed externally on roof or above quarter lights, painted white with black letters (or cream with chocolate letters).				
BUILDERS' PLATES	Black with white letters, etc.				

TABLES 5, 5A - CARRIAGE INTERIORS

TABLE 5 CARRIAGE INTERIORS [1]	First Class	Third Class
UPHOLSTERY	Blue moquette velvet, buttoned through, including door panels.	Autumn Tint, gold/grey rep cloth.
WOODWORK	Walnut, sycamore, etc., panelled and polished.	Stained and varnished.
FITTINGS, etc.	Bevelled mirrors, polished metal, blue carpet.	Plain fittings, brown linoleum with HR pattern.
BRAKE COMPARTMENTS	Stained wood walls, white ceilings, black ironwork.	
The information given is confirmed for later periods only. See also Plates 12 and 37 for interior of a passenger coach door.		

TABLE 5A CARRIAGE INTERIORS [1]	Sleeping Cars Nos. 8 and 9	Excursion Saloons Nos. 195 and 196
CORRIDOR LINING	Varnished Cypress.	Not applicable.
COMPARTMENT / SALOON LINING - 3rd and attendants	Varnished figured pitched pine.	Varnished figured pitched pine, with teak mouldings and fascias.
SEATS - 3rd Class	Rep cloth.	Rep cloth.
SLEEPING COMPARTMENT	Finished white, teak mouldings, tapestry upholstery.	Not applicable.
SLIDING DOORS in CORRIDOR	Varnished Teak.	Not applicable.
SLEEPING COMPARTMENT COMMUNICATION DOORS	Varnished teak, with "massive" bevelled mirror each side on top panel.	Not applicable.
The information given is from a contemporary description.		

'Skye Bogie' No. 48 at Fort Augustus. Built in December 1901 almost twenty years after the first of the class, No. 48 worked the Invergarry and Fort Augustus Railway during much of the Highland's tenure from 1903 to 1907.

[from a painting by George F. Heiron

A rare example of an original transfer of the full Highland Railway Crest. The Coat of Arms was adopted upon the formation of the Highland Railway Company in 1865, the heraldic description being: an Eagle displayed, bearing two shields, charged with the arms of the City of Perth (Gules, the Holy Lamb passant regardant, argent, carrying a banner of St. Andrew, proper, within a double tressure flory-counter, argent) and the Burgh of Inverness (Gules, our Lord upon the Cross, proper). The Coat of Arms is surrounded by a garter, together making the full crest.

To be heraldically correct, the object within the garter should not be called a Coat of Arms, since it was not granted by The Court of the Lord Lyon, the body in Scotland responsible for such things. The HR Co., in common with many other railways and commercial undertakings, simply took it upon itself to proclaim its self-given status. Instead, it might be more properly called an Armourial Device.

In this book, the total emblem is called a Crest, the inner object a Coat of Arms, and the surround a Garter. *[original transfer from late Gavin Wilson collection*

Plate 47. The 'Jones Goods' No. 103 at Perth in August 1964. *[HMRS collection AAA 151*

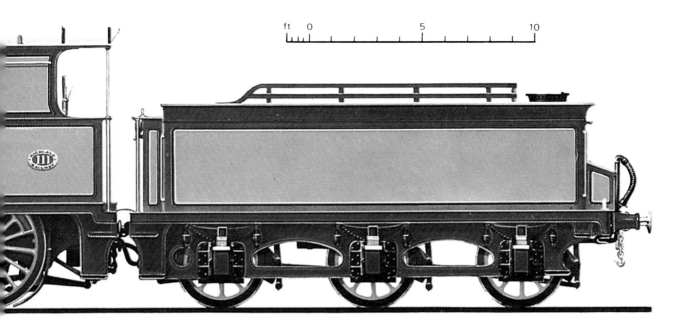

Plate 48. Jones 'Big Goods' Class 4-6-0 No. 111 in full two-tone Jones II Green livery – a reproduction of a colour painting by Arthur Wolstenholme which appeared originally in LocoProfile 17 *Jones Goods & Indian L*. The caption stated that this was "the only authentic record of pre-1898 colouring and lining". We leave the reader to study the colour plates, and to make up his own mind as to what the "right" colour might have been.

[Howard Geddes collection

Plate 49. Jones 'Big Goods' Class 4-6-0 No. 115 in full two-tone Jones II green livery – a reproduction of a water-colour painting by Maurice Secretan, originally published in the July 1936 edition of *The Railway Magazine*. In that issue, JN Maskelyne stated that this painting could be accepted as being correct in every detail. However, C Hamilton Ellis has stated that when it first appeared he had been informed by Mary Beals-Jones, the daughter of David Jones himself, that the green was the wrong colour and that the correct shade was that of an F Moore (LPC) original oil painting that she owned.[14] This actual oil painting (or an identical copy thereof) is reproduced on the front cover. It should be noted that Secretan had been a painter under the F Moore label; it is not known who painted No. 116, although it is not beyond the bounds of possibility that it was Secretan.   *[Courtesy Railway Magazine*

[14]   Information provided by Neil Sinclair, from conversation with C Hamilton Ellis at the Highland Railway Centenary exhibition in 1965. OS Nock tells a slightly different story in his *The Highland Railway*, p60, but draws the conclusion, incorrectly in the light of the above, that perhaps the "correct" colour was Improved Engine Green.

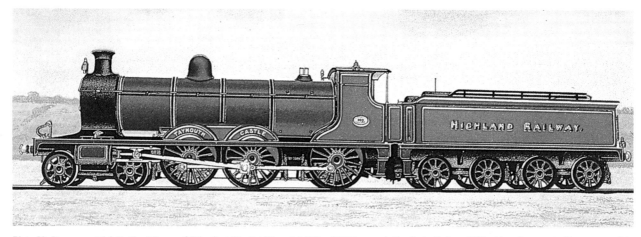

Plate 50. Drummond I fully-lined livery. Of the first 'Castle' Class 4-6-0 No. 140 *Taymouth Castle*, built June 1900, this colour study first appeared in February 1902 *Railway Magazine* whilst the livery was still current, in support of an extensive description of Lochgorm works.

Plate 51. Drummond II plain livery. Of the first 'Big Ben' Class 4-4-0 No. 61 *Ben na Caillich*, built May 1908, this colour study first appeared in December 1908 *Railway Magazine*, whilst the livery was still current. A photograph taken of the locomotive in works grey which had previously appeared in the June 1908 issue was clearly the basis on which the painting was produced (even though the locomotive was announced as Ben na Gaillich!).

Plate 52. Cumming livery. Of the namesake Class 4-4-0 No. 73 *Snaigow*, built November 1916, this colour study first appeared in February 1917 *Railway Magazine*. A photograph taken of the locomotive when new which had previously appeared in the January 1917 issue was clearly the basis on which the painting was produced. Plate 71 is of this same photograph.

Given that all three prints were produced contemporaneously with their subject, and many years apart, it is striking that the three greens are all very similar. However, since they were all painted from photographs, with perhaps the painter not having seen the actual locomotives, there can be no claim that the shades of green are accurate.

[all three transparencies by David Stirling,
from original magazines kindly provided by Railway Enthusiast Club,
reproduced with permission from Railway Magazine.

CHAPTER 3 - NON-PASSENGER COACHING STOCK

This Chapter discusses goods vehicles whose primary purpose was not to carry passengers but which were painted similarly to regular coaching stock, rather than taking the standard goods vehicle livery. The Highland did not classify vehicles in this way. As we shall see, there is considerable doubt about the scope of application of this passenger livery to these vehicles.

A key feature of this classification of vehicle is that they were constructed to run in passenger trains. In earlier days, this may have been little more than construction to passenger vehicle technical specification, which would be more advanced than that of ordinary goods vehicles, e.g. as basic as using sprung buffers and drawgear rather than dumb buffers. There would be no physical reason why vehicles of any type should not be intermixed.

Later, compatibility of braking systems became important, initially perhaps no more than the provision of external communication cord loops. As safety arrangements advanced, passenger and goods vehicles became sufficiently incompatible that many could not be intermixed. Non-passenger coaching stock had a foot in both camps.

The Highland's use of Newall's mechanical continuous brake meant that those non-passenger vehicles with that gear were confined to similarly-braked passenger trains, and could not travel in loose-coupled trains. There is a suggestion that these vehicles were identified by number only, and not by livery or other external design feature. On the other hand, hand-braked vehicles could run on passenger trains, to a certain extent.

As the vacuum automatic brake superseded the mechanical brake in the 1890s, goods vehicles fell into three categories:

- **fitted**: vehicles with continuous brakes, either vacuum or Westinghouse or both. They were confined to passenger trains or to running immediately behind the engine on goods trains.
- **piped**: vehicles with hand-brakes and through brake pipes. They could run on passenger trains, although they did not contribute to the automatic braking capacity.
- **unfitted**: vehicles with hand-brakes only. They would not normally run on passenger trains, although if they did, they would have to be hung on at the rear.

It appears that fitted vehicles were intended for the conveyance of articles and animals charged at passenger rather than goods rates, and would normally run on passenger trains. Piped vehicles were intended to be capable of running on passenger trains or goods trains, according to circumstances. Unfitted vehicles were the bread-and-butter of the railway.

Example of fitted and piped vehicle are:

- Horse Boxes - fitted.
- Open Carriage Trucks - fitted.
- Close Carriage Trucks (including Motor Car Vans) - fitted.
- Valuable Cattle Vans - piped.
- Cattle Trucks - some 25 were piped; the rest unfitted.
- Meat Vans - authorities differ whether they were all fitted, all piped, or a mixture. The earliest Meat Vans might even have been unfitted, and hence treated as ordinary goods vehicles.
- Close Luggage Vans - some fitted, some unfitted. These vehicles (all four-wheeled) should not be confused with passenger brake vans of all varieties, despite that they were lettered as Luggage Vans. Those that were fitted, were transferred to passenger stock in 1912 and counted together with the passenger brake vans.
- Covered Goods Vans - some were fitted when built or converted later; otherwise, unfitted. See comments below.
- Fish Trucks - pre-1902 builds were piped only; post-1902 builds only were fitted. All were transferred to passenger stock in 1912.

Some vehicles were converted to or built with steam heating facilities, but this did not determine whether a vehicle was fitted or piped.

It seems that some fitted or piped vehicles were treated as ordinary goods vehicles, liveried as in Chapter 4. This is likely the case with early goods vehicles which were piped or fitted later in life, and never repainted nor re-designated. It is also likely that Covered Goods Vans were treated thus; one may in fact go so far as to suggest that the distinction between Close Luggage Vans and Covered Goods Vans was that by definition the former were honoured with the passenger livery, the latter not. The fitted Covered Goods Vans were available as back-up luggage vans during the heavy summer season. The unfitted Close Luggage Vans were presumably early stock that latterly may have pottered about in the far north or were downgraded to ordinary goods van duties.

There is a more fundamental doubt, however, about the application of passenger livery to non-passenger coaching stock.

The following were classed as passenger stock and generally ran in passenger trains. Hence, there is general agreement that these were passenger-green liveried. Note that they were all fully fitted vehicles.

- Horse Boxes
- Carriage Trucks (open and closed)
- latterly, Fish Trucks and Luggage Vans

But it is felt in some quarters that there is both photographic and documentary evidence that, whilst circumstantial, indicates that vehicles that normally ran in goods trains, whether fitted, piped or unfitted, were painted the same, namely red-oxide not green. For instance, documentation from the 1880s to 1920 uses either vehicle numbers or presence of vacuum cylinders to identify passenger-rated vehicles, and never their colour. And study of certain photographs seems to indicate that fish trucks

previously thought to be green are in fact a different colour to that of a nearby engine which is known to be in green livery.

Thus, there are doubts about several of the categories above. On the one hand, it is reasonable to infer that the Cattle Trucks were not painted green, but on the other hand every published source states that Meat Vans were green. One theory is that in Jones' time, all such goods vehicles were painted red-oxide and by and large remained so even when converted, whereas Drummond and on tended to paint new stock green if fitted or (less-likely) if piped. Thus, there was a long transitional period where both types of livery may have existed side by side. There is insufficient evidence to prove the case either way.

The amount of available information is extremely sparse and rather confusing: more - especially different vehicle type descriptions and passenger/goods livery examples - would be welcome. These comments apply equally to the next two chapters on Goods and Non-Revenue Earning Vehicles. A suggested source is extreme enlargements of photographs of the George Washington Wilson Collection at Aberdeen University, although the cost does makes blanket or speculative enlargements expensive.

Plate 53. Illiteracy symbol on Diagram 5 (Type H) wagon No. 2630: a 10 ton six-plank dumb-buffered Loco Coal wagon apparently with no side doors. The photograph seems to have been taken early in Drummond's regime. The number as shown may be the only identification on the side - very small compared with what one would normally expect for standard Drummond livery. It is also possible that, in line with other companies, the illiteracy symbol and the number appeared in the equivalent position on the top right of the wagon side.

[Howard Geddes collection

TABLE 6 - NON-PASSENGER COACHING STOCK

TABLE 6 NON-PASSENGER COACHING STOCK	All periods
BODY SIDES, ENDS, SOLEBARS, BUFFER BEAMS	Coaching stock green [1]
ROOFS (ex-works only)	White (except 1902/3-1912: mid-grey)
RUNNING & BRAKE GEAR, STEPS, HANDRAILS, etc.	Black
ALL OTHER IRONWORK	Black
WHEELS	Black, with white tyres.
SOLEBAR NUMBER and WEIGHT PLATES	Cast with numbers raised up. Painted black, with white letters.
INSIGNIA	
FISH and MEAT VANS	Yellow, block, plain
ALL OTHER VEHICLES	Yellow, block, shaded black to lower right
LETTER and NUMERAL SIZES	These all varied according to the type and size of the vehicle to which they were applied, as below.
COMPANY LETTERS	The height of the **H R** lettering was:- • 1896-1904: 12" after 1904: 15" on van sides • 4" on carriage truck side rails • generally "two planks" on fish trucks
FLEET No. NUMERALS	The height of numerals was:- • often 4", but also from 7" to 9" (or "one plank") on sides. The positions varied. • approx. 4" high on ends
TARE WEIGHT	Tare Weight numerals were 3" high.

TABLE 6 NON-PASSENGER COACHING STOCK	**All periods**
VEHICLE TYPE DESCRIPTION LETTERS	Letters as in **FISH**, **MEAT**, etc. were usually 9" high. Vehicle type descriptions such as **HORSE BOX** **MEAT VAN** **CARRIAGE TRUCK** **MOTOR CAR VAN** **FISH TRAFFIC** **LUGGAGE VAN** [2] were applied to each side. Not all carriage trucks had such descriptions applied, nor did any Covered Goods Vans or Cattle Trucks, as far as is known. It is not known whether the two Valuable Cattle Vans were lettered, nor whether all Luggage Vans were so lettered.

[1]   If it were accepted that stock was in fact painted red-oxide with white lettering, then it follows that stock transferred to the passenger lists in 1912 (Fish Trucks and Close Luggage Vans) is likely to have been re-painted green.

[2]   These would be the fitted versions. See also footnote in Table 7.

9"

Figure 7. Drawing of illiteracy symbol, based on available photographs.   *[Simon de Souza*

CHAPTER 4 - GOODS VEHICLES

The details in this Chapter cover ordinary revenue-earning goods vehicles, normally not fitted with an automatic brake system or even through pipes. This scope includes goods brake vans.

Vehicles appearing in freshly-painted condition would be much less frequent than would usually be the case for passenger-carrying and other fitted stock. Hence, the livery as specified would appear mainly on wagons that were new or freshly overhauled. Over time, paint would almost disappear from the wooden parts of ordinary wagons, with minor repairs left unpainted, and ironwork rusty. However, goods brake vans were generally kept in better condition.

Cattle trucks and sheep wagons would quickly have become quite unsightly, having been subjected to lime washes after use. Lime washing was also required for horse boxes that had been used (quite legitimately) for cattle and sheep as well as horses, and even to goods brake vans after use by horses. However, it may be reasonably assumed that these vehicles were kept clean and tidy.

As discussed in the previous Chapter, some or all vehicles which were through-piped or fully-fitted may have been painted in the goods red-oxide rather than the passenger green. If that were the case, these vehicles, particularly Covered Goods Vans but also Meat Vans, are covered by this Chapter.

Some of these wagons, e.g. Meat Vans, may have been varnished, and thus clearly would have remained smarter for longer.

Plate 54. Jones Type C (Diagram 6) "open-box" 8 ton wagon No. 2462, taken at Barmouth in 1924, showing the standard Drummond lettering style on the side and still with the Jones-style number plate on the solebar. A close-up of a Jones number plate is given in Plate 60.
[HMRS collection AK608

TABLE 7 - GOODS VEHICLES

TABLE 7 GOODS VEHICLES	All periods
BODY SIDES, ENDS, SOLEBARS, BUFFER BEAMS	Claret until 1896, then rich red-oxide.
ROOFS (ex-works only)	White (except 1902/3-1912: mid-grey)
RUNNING & BRAKE GEAR	Black
ALL OTHER IRONWORK	Black
WHEELS	Black, with white tyres, only when new.
SOLEBAR NUMBER and WEIGHT PLATES	Cast with numbers raised up. Painted black, with white letters. See Plate 85.
INSIGNIA: JONES period	
LETTERS and NUMERALS	Wagons carried only a large number plate on each solebar, giving the wagon number, the owning company and the load weight, there being no large wagon-side lettering or numbering. See Plates 54, 60 and 85.
ILLITERACY SYMBOL	Many wagons carried an illiteracy symbol. This consisted of a relatively small circle, within which there were two overlapping shields, one white and one yellow. The yellow shield was overlapped by the white shield; the vertical axis of the yellow shield was skewed some 20° to the left; that of the white shield, to the right. Within the yellow shield was an **H** and within the white shield was an **R**, both letters in claret. See Plates 53 and 59, and Figure 7. [1]
INSIGNIA: DRUMMOND onwards	
LETTER and NUMERAL APPLICATION	Plain white lettering and numerals were applied, see Plate 56. [2] Their size varied according to the type and size of the vehicle to which they were applied, as below. The insignia were also applied to pre-Drummond stock, probably when the wagons were either repaired or repainted rather than to a specific programme. There appears to have been one or more interim hybrid arrangements of insignia between the time of Drummond's appointment and the time his standard livery became established, possibly as late as 1904. However, photographic evidence is insufficient to confidently identify the trends.
COMPANY LETTER SIZES	The letters **H** and **R** were always applied symmetrically about the vertical centre-line of the vehicle, their height tending to be:- ♦ 1896-1904: 12"; after 1904: 15" on wagon and van sides. ♦ generally "two planks" (12") on open wagons, but also "three planks" which works out at 18" high. ♦ 9" on cattle trucks (on top plank on either side of the door) and sheep vans (in similar position, on boards specially provided for the purpose in front of the bars of the circus-cage type of double-deck sheep van) It is possible that as one of the hybrid arrangements, Drummond continued to rely on the illiteracy symbol instead of the company letters. The style (font) of the company letters remained fairly constant throughout.

TABLE 7 GOODS VEHICLES	All periods
FLEET No. NUMERALS SIZE and POSITION	The height of numerals was:- ♦ often 4", but sometimes from 7" to 9" (or "one plank") on wagon and van sides, especially on goods brake vans where they may have been as large as 12". ♦ approx. 4" high on wagon and van ends ♦ 3" high underneath the illiteracy symbol where present As Drummond's style took time to settle down, the earliest application of painted fleet numbers would have been in 3" high numerals under the symbol. The 4" size probably followed next, typically on the lower left of each side, second plank up, above the Tare Weight. The larger 7" numerals seemed to have come into effect somewhat later and the 9" numerals later still. Most photographs show them on loco coal wagons, with their position varying seemingly randomly: sometimes lower right, lower left and top centre. In a well-known photograph of a new meat van, the number appears only on the van's ends, there being no number on the van's side. It is not known whether this is significant.
TARE WEIGHT	Numerals were 3" high, separated by full-stops, and were generally placed on the bottom left of each side: thus: 13 · 11 · 0 or 13 . 11
ILLITERACY SYMBOL	Continued to be applied until 1903. In addition, the vehicle number was applied underneath. It is not known whether this number was instead of or in addition to the full-size vehicle-side numbers.
VEHICLE TYPE DESCRIPTION LETTERS	Letters as in **MEAT**, etc. were usually 9" high, but there were great variations. In particular, loco coal wagons had great differences. If present, vehicle type descriptions such as **LOCO COAL** or **LOCO. COAL** or **LOCO COAL ONLY** or even **Loco Coal** **MEAT VAN** **ROAD VAN GOODS** or **ROAD VAN** **LUGGAGE VAN** [3] were applied to each side, usually symmetrically. However, some loco coal wagons had their descriptors in condensed lettering low down and on the left side of the wagon side.
OTHER INSIGNIA	Other items appeared on various vehicles at differing times. Information is too scarce for any meaningful analysis, so more would be welcome. Standard manufacturers plates were applied. If present on neither a solebar number plate nor the manufacturer's plate, the maximum load for the vehicle was painted on the vehicle itself, in the same size and style as the Tare Weight, but at the other end, thus: **LOAD 10 TONS**

TABLE 7 GOODS VEHICLES	All periods
OTHER INSIGNIA (contd.)	Called "fitted-ups", open wagons converted to carry sheep had triangular marks in white on the sides at each end, positioned it is thought at the top of the corner strapping and the outer edge of the wagon. Such a wagon could be fitted-up with a removable flake, which looked like a fence on stilts, ensuring that the sheep were secure in the wagon by raising the effective height of the wagon sides. The flakes themselves tended to be temporary, simply unpainted timber, or perhaps creosoted. In use, they would soon take on a white appearance, being lime-washed along with the rest of the interior of the wagon to which they were fitted.
GOODS BRAKE VANS	These were finished as for unfitted wagons, but the shade of red was reportedly much richer, perhaps because they were varnished and embellished by the men to whom they were allocated. See Plate 58. The *Locomotive Magazine* has these vans as dark lake, yellow lettering shaded red, and vermilion ends. It is also reported that the interiors were light buff. Vans were lettered variously, in letters approximately 6" high, apart from when the letters were on the guard's ogee where they were 3". **GOODS BRAKE** **ROAD VAN GOODS** [4] **ROAD VAN** and often had a black board giving the guard's name and his home station in white letters. It is likely that some brake vans, those that had regular routes, had their route announced on the side, e.g. **PERTH & FORRES** Lettering was sometimes on the lookout, sometimes just either side and sometimes widely spaced. Typically, the **H R** was large (12" or 15") with the number slightly smaller (7" or 9", but maybe also 12").
	With the guard's ogee in the middle of the van, examples of relative positioning were as follows: 1896-1907: H GOODS BRAKE X X R Post-1907: GOODS H R / X X BRAKE
	With the guard's ogee at one end, more variations were apparent: H R X X GOODS BRAKE the **GOODS** and **BRAKE** being under windows. H R X X GOODS BRAKE all the lettering being between windows - see Plate 55.

TABLE 7 GOODS VEHICLES	All periods

1. There is a photograph which shows, in the background of a shot of Big Goods No. 116, Loco Coal wagon No. 2630 with the symbol together with Drummond's large lettering. This demonstrates that the illiteracy symbols continued into Drummond's time. A much enlarged fragment is shown in Plate 53 showing the detail of the symbol. According to one authority, these illiteracy symbols may have appeared on Locomotive Department vehicles (i.e. non-revenue) only. See also Plate 62.

2. However, there is evidence that in some circumstances or on some occasions shaded lettering and numbering was used - see Plate 57.

3. Known as Close Luggage Vans, these would be un-fitted versions, which at least latterly were not allowed on passenger trains between Perth and Inverness. Conversely, vacuum-fitted versions were not allowed on "the goods circuit". The 1920 Appendix distinguishes the two types of vehicle by reference to the presence or absence of the vacuum cylinder, not the livery, which adds to the evidence that all were painted in the same livery: that of ordinary goods vehicles.

4. The six-wheel brake vans were roomy and were used for carrying parcels and sundry goods items: they were generally referred to as Road Vans. Although these brake vans were known as Road Vans, it is thought unlikely that they were so liveried. However, Sir Eric Hutchison has written (in *Railway Modeller* July 1954) that some of the big six-wheelers definitely were.

Drummond built some vehicles specially designated as Road Vans to Diagram 31 (goods series); these matchboarded vehicles were almost identical to his 1902 Diagram 38 (passenger series) six-wheel panelled passenger brake vans with four roof lights, except they had only simple handbrakes, were without guards' facilities, and hence lacked guards' ogees. The Diagram 31 vehicles were probably all liveried as Road Van or Road Van Goods. They can be regarded as ordinary un-fitted goods vehicles. The 1922 Working Timetable shows at least one working on an ordinary goods train between Lairg and Inverness, being picked up by the train ex-Wick. It is likely that these Road Vans simply provided additional and more flexible capacity than goods brake vans.

Refer to Plate 33 of a passenger brake van for a guide as to what a Road Van looked like. Of course, Plate 33 shows a passenger brake van liveried as a Luggage Van, as were other passenger brake vans; it is not known whether the four-wheel covered luggage vans (Diagram 8 and similar) were also liveried as Luggage Vans! However, as already stated, after 1912, fitted Close Luggage Vans and Passenger Brake Vans were counted together.

Plate 55. A delightful study at Fochabers Town, with a mixed train just arrived. The goods portion consists of two open wagons and a brake van. The **R** can just be made out on the unsheeted wagon. The brake van is No. 6 which was rated at 10-tons. It was a Type A (Diagram 24) van, built 1900. Note that the van is at least piped, if not actually fitted. These vans were commonly called Klondykes, presumably after the gold-rush to the Klondyke River in the Yukon in 1896. Interestingly, it was around this time that the line to Kyle was finally opened, giving access to market for the great herring fleets. The herring fishery itself became known as the klondyke, and to this day Russian factory ships are known as klondykers. Although the connection is there, quite why these brake vans in particular should have become known as Klondykes is not clear.
[Howard Geddes collection

Plate 56. Drummond-era 16-ton Loco Coal wagon to Diagram 33 of 1904. One can just glimpse the position of the numbering on the ends - third plank down. The design follows that of the Caledonian. Fifty were built by Hurst Nelson for £84 each.

[HMRS Hurst Nelson collection T14-14

Plate 57. Drummond-era 10-ton covered van No. 1168 of 1912, built by RY Pickering for £120 to a similar design of van built at Inverness in 1907 and 1918. Note the shaded insignia. The 1907 vans had vacuum brakes fitted; if this were true of the 1912 batch, this may explain the "posh" insignia. There is no sign of pipes nor vacuum fitments; on the other hand there is no sign of a hand brake either. Given the presence of the ratchet for a hand-brake, one wonders if this van was in fact only partially built. Note that the axle-box appears to be dated 1911, the year before recorded delivery to the Highland.

[Peter Tatlow collection

Plate 58. Cumming-era 20-ton brake van to the 1918 batch of Diagram 38. These had a steel underframe.

[HMRS Pickering collection WX11

WAGON SHEETS

Wagon sheets were used to cover loads in open wagons. They were made of water-proof black tarpaulin, around 21 feet by 14 feet in size.

They were subject to the same accounting arrangements as the wagons themselves as far as the Railway Clearing House was concerned. Mileage and demurrage were charged on wagon sheets in their own right. Hence, if for no other reason, it was essential they be readily identified.

A specimen layout of letters and numbers is set out in Figure 8. Doubtless there were other formats.

All lettering and numbers were white.

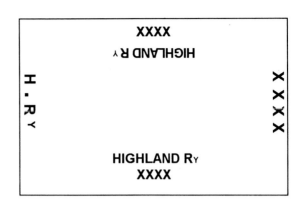

Figure 8. Example of the layout of lettering on a wagon sheet. Not to scale. *[Howard Geddes]*

Plate 59. Illiteracy symbol on wagon No. 1328 (or 1326): a four-plank 8 ton open to Diagram 1 (Type A). Although suspected that the wagon is being used as a Loco Department Sand Wagon, this plate could be evidence that ordinary open wagons, not just department wagons, had the illiteracy symbol.

[Howard Geddes collection

WAGON ROPES

Even the ropes used in securing loads were subject to Railway Clearing House rules and charges, in the same way as Wagon Sheets. These ropes had any mark that the owning company might think fit to identify the rope's owner, which was typically by means of one or more strands being dyed certain colours. This was hardly satisfactory, and from July 1861, it was required that a metal ferule stamped with the company initials be attached to the middle of each rope.

The author is not aware of the Highland's arrangements.

As an aside, the Inverness & Aberdeen Junction Railway was a member of the RCH by 31 December 1860, presumably from the time connection with the south was made at Keith in 1858. The Inverness & Nairn Railway was not a member.

PRIVATE OWNER WAGONS

The Highland Railway did not have very many indigenous examples of traders running privately-owned wagons, whether as private owners running their own wagons or as private traders running hired or leased wagons from other sources.

The traders and their wagons are detailed by Richard White and Peter Tatlow in the *HMRS Journal Vol. 14 No. 8 (1992)*. All seem to have been supplied by Hurst, Nelson & Co., Motherwell, or R.Y. Pickering & Co., Wishaw. Most were registered with the Highland, some with the Caledonian and one or two were from even further afield, e.g. CA Miller & Sons had one each registered with the GWR and L&YR.

All were open or mineral wagons, ranging from the most primitive dumb-buffered examples to more up to date types. All traders handled coal, although some dealt in other bulk commodities such as lime and potatoes.

Three examples of livery are known to the author, although there may be others recorded.

- JS MacPherson, Kingussie: red-oxide body, white lettering shaded black.

- CA Miller & Sons, Pitlochry: lake body, white lettering, white tyres.

- Marshall, Blair Atholl: red-oxide body, white lettering shaded black, white tyres.

All had black ironwork.

As far as is known, there were no other types of privately-owned wagons, except perhaps for six refrigerated Fish Vans built for The Fish League by the Swansea Wagon Co. which ran briefly in 1883. No other details are known, and in any event it is doubtful that these can be regarded as indigenous.

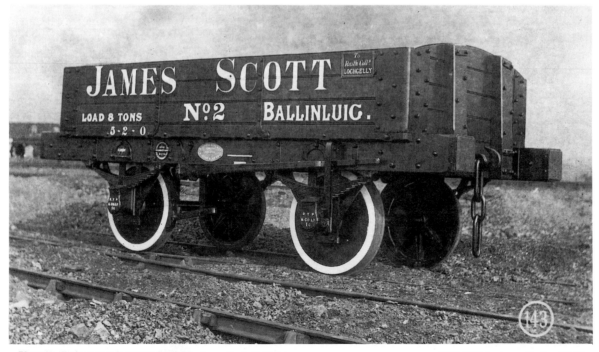

Plate 61. Early wagon, by RY Pickering for James Scott, Ballinluig.   *[HMRS Pickering collection W143*

CHAPTER 5 - NON-REVENUE EARNING VEHICLES

The details in this Chapter cover all those vehicles and appliances associated with the upkeep of the physical plant of the railway. Although such as ballast wagons and special-purpose vehicles were generally purchased new, other wagons and vans and some personnel-carrying vehicles were usually rebuilt or adapted from wagons and coaches that had previously been withdrawn from revenue earning service. One odd construction was a portable stone-breaker built at Lochgorm, consisting of a crusher, engine and bothy mounted on a bogie wagon; this was often kept in quarry sidings.

At certain places on the HR, the more common fixed goods yard crane was supplemented or substituted by a mobile version. This was a more-or-less standard yard crane mounted on an old 4 or 6 wheel flat truck which could either roam the yard or work only on a short stub of track on a loading platform. For the purpose of classification, these are included in this chapter.

Details such are as available are given in Table 8 *Non-revenue Earning Vehicles*, which covers:-

- ◆ Coaches and vans
- ◆ Wagons and trucks
- ◆ Mobile yard hand cranes
- ◆ Breakdown and travelling cranes, both hand and steam powered
- ◆ Snowploughs, etc.

A 10-ton hand **breakdown crane** was kept at Lochgorm. On a six-wheel dumb-buffered chassis, the one known photograph gives no clue to the livery. Apparently, the crane was written-off sometime before 1923 by falling down a rocky bank near Carrbridge.

The **Inverness breakdown train** was reported as running at one time in locomotive green. Plate 62 shows it to be fully lined out, in either white or yellow lines against a darker border, suggesting the adoption of locomotive livery style. The crane was built by Cowans Sheldon in 1887 and was of 15-ton capacity. [15] There is a story that the crane was destined for a railway in India but the order was cancelled, so the Highland got the cancelled crane at a bargain price, even having it altered to suit. Certainly the crane was non-standard with some features otherwise unknown in Britain but common abroad, and was substantial to say the least for the size of the Highland, at a time when hand-cranes were still commonplace on much larger railways.

Plate 62. The Inverness breakdown train, very smartly turned out in what appears to be Jones locomotive livery. The wagons and van are lettered **H.R LOCO DEPT**. The two wagons have the illiteracy symbol on their top left of side. A later photograph of only the crane and match wagon shows the crane unlined with **H.R** on the coal bunker and **H.R. LOCO DEPT** on the match wagon. *[Real Photographs 14443*

---

[15]   *Railway Steam Cranes* by John S Brownlie, published by the author 1973, covers the subject comprehensively. There is a fine photograph of the crane as built, as well as details of its facilities and operation. For those interested, a scale drawing of the crane appeared in the *Model Railway Constructor* for July 1970.

Nonetheless, it was severely damaged when it too fell down an embankment, this time near Etteridge Crossing in 1894.

The **mobile yard cranes** carried neither fleet numbers, company lettering nor tare weights, since they rarely left their home yard. They were simply signwritten on the solebar, e.g.

Thurso Crane

Their livery can hardly have been the usual claret; but there is no known photograph showing a crane in any livery apart from "filthy".

TABLE 8 **NON-REVENUE EARNING VEHICLES**	**All periods**
BODY SIDES, ENDS, SOLEBARS, BUFFER BEAMS	Claret (but see note about cranes, above).
ROOFS OF VANS	White (except 1902/3-1912: mid-grey)
RUNNING and BRAKE GEAR	Black
INSIGNIA	Yellow, unshaded. Sizes as for revenue stock. Ballast wagons may have been lettered **P. WAY. DEPT.** in large letters, sometime after 1901. If so, it is likely that this came into effect with Drummond's 1904 insignia changes.
ALL OTHER IRONWORK	Black

Plate 63. A pleasant view of Garve, showing the station nameboard and the station building with white woodwork, darker (burnt-sienna with purple-brown edging?) finial and bargeboards. Notice also the trunking covering the wiring from the telegraph pole down and around the wall and into the building itself: this was a common feature. A couple of hurlies are prominent; on the nearer, the station name can just be made out painted on the shaft. Although taken in LMS times, little has changed since Highland days.   *[Lens of Sutton*

CHAPTER 6 - LINESIDE

This Chapter covers fixed plant on and along the route of the railway. Research has been made easier by two factors: the longevity of the applied colours due to the lack of atmospheric pollution in the Highlands, and the continuation by the LMS of many of the basic painting schemes and hues.

Railway-owned structures such as hotels, workmen's cottages and other such buildings are not covered. Neither are structures, vehicles or equipment owned by others (e.g. carters, lessees, contractors), even when they were used exclusively in the pursuance of railway business.

BUILDINGS

Highland Railway station buildings constructed from masonry varied somewhat from one location to another, according to the importance of the station and the facilities provided, but most of them exhibited similar characteristics, and all were unpainted.

Those constructed from timber were much more standardised, being constructed from one basic set of plans and having two, one or no end gables according to status. Many of the late 19th and early 20th century structures appear to have been assembled from parts prefabricated at Inverness. This most certainly is the case in respect of signal cabins, goods sheds, passenger waiting shelters, and permanent way and motive power depot huts, etc. The small station buildings at Dornoch and Lybster, and the additional structure at The Mound Junction, appear to have been built from the same set of plans, as do the branch engine sheds at the above two termini, Lybster having better ventilation.

The type of timber used for main walls was larch, to which the main wall colour of burnt-sienna for buildings used by the public was complementary. Signal Cabins were also painted burnt-sienna, presumably being deemed worthy of such treatment. Corner posts and similar beams were painted purple-brown, as were doors. Virtually all other buildings were simply creosoted. However, small goods stores of the sort often found on loading banks appear to have been painted, although this was not universally the case.

According to Sir Eric Hutchison, a major livery change occurred after 1912, with the upper parts of station and signal cabin walls and water columns being in a light-stone colour with the lower three

feet remaining burnt-sienna, the two colours being separated by a one inch black line; water tank panels were claimed to be infilled cream or stone instead of burnt-sienna. This has been interpreted as the change actually coming into effect from 1912. However, all photographic evidence points towards a single livery throughout Highland ownership. Given that Sir Eric is on record as saying that he saw nothing of the Highland between 1912 and 1926, it is likely that he was meaning that the change happened sometime after he last saw the Highland in 1912. The current consensus is that the change to the two-tone livery occurred much later - actually in LMS days, indeed as late as 1936: see Chapter 10. As a final word on the supposed two-tone livery, a well-known 1880's photograph of both goods shed and all-timber, all-over roofed passenger terminal at Strome Ferry shows the lower three feet as dark and all above as light. This can be safely discounted as support to the two-tone theory, the dark base being simply unpainted masonry, not discernible as such in the photograph.

Another doubtful point concerns the colour of window frames, sashes and glazing bars on all station and associated structures, including signal cabins. A study of many photographs shows these were either white or purple-brown. As an example, the almost identical station buildings at Buckie and Fortrose, photographed only one year apart, show white windows on the former and purple-brown on the latter, whilst the light railway termini and junction buildings mentioned above had the purple-brown applied to windows when new in 1902/3.

As far as is known, virtually all goods sheds were creosoted on the main walls, the windows and doors being painted burnt-sienna. Photos taken around 1880 of Blair Atholl show an all-over apparently white shed. A possible, but not entirely convincing, explanation is that a freshly creosoted building has a glossy sheen, and can thus give the impression of being either painted or very lightly coloured, depending on how the light is reflected. However, some branch line goods sheds, especially the gable-end types as at Fortrose and Dornoch, were painted all over to match the station buildings' paint scheme. It is known that Strome Ferry shed was so painted, as was perhaps Thurso. Finally, scrapings from two goods sheds, one at Lybster, had both grey and green shades of paint in their various layers, although it cannot be stated with certainty that these were applied in Highland days.

Locomotive sheds, water tank bases, permanent way cabins and other structures not regarded as public buildings, were finished as for goods sheds, except that masonry was left untouched. Where an old coach or van body was used as a store or mess room (and this was quite common), it was probably repainted plain coach green, unlettered, before delivery from Inverness to the site. Plate 66 of Lybster locomotive shed exhibits a glossy finish, probably of fresh creosote, but looking very much like fresh gloss paint.

SIGNALLING

McKenzie & Holland Ltd. of Worcester was the major supplier to the Highland Railway, which in the main followed their supplier's standard practices. However, the products of Dutton and Co., also of Worcester, were fitted north of Inverness at certain locations, and at Keith East. The signalling at Kyle was, unusually for the Highland, supplied by The Railway Signalling Co. (Fazakerly).

SIGNAL LADDERS

It has often been stated that the Highland Railway did not use signal ladders (due to the lamps being on windlass gear, thus enabling them to be maintained from ground level), and that any ladders, other than on bracketed signal posts, were added by the LMS. However, recent publications have clearly revealed that, well before LMS days, signal ladders were in evidence on signal posts at Forres, The Mound, Clachnaharry and Kyle of Lochalsh. Although not climbed every day, they were still required for maintenance purposes.

Ladders were also evident on the high posts carrying signal wires, where these posts carried angle cranks, balance weights, etc. At the exit from certain sidings where sighting was difficult, e.g. Inverness Rose Street, Blair Atholl loco shed and Killiecrankie, standard revolving ground signals were mounted on tall hollow cast iron columns, complete with ladder.

Plate 64. Junction signal on the approaches to Inverness, amidst a veritable forest of signals and poles. Taken around the time of the grouping, note that the distant arms are still red. See how the signal wires are taken off the signal at mid-height, leading straight across the tracks to a signal wire post. Unusually, the signal post appears to be white from ground up, unlike the shunt signal on the far left. The miniature signal is of Midland Rly. origin, possibly installed during WWI.

[David Stirling collection, courtesy AJ Lambert

SHUNT SIGNALS

The semaphore bow-tie shunt signals sometimes had a blank plate fitted in the lower spectacle, with a cut out "S" showing white. Others are reported as being left open (i.e. no glass nor plate, showing a white light when "off"). However, some good quality photos of Kyle shunt signals show a normal glass in the "green" spectacle.

Early shunt signals had a single red spectacle with an "S" shaped plate in the lamp glass.

SIGNAL WIRE POSTS

It is perhaps worthwhile noting that the posts used to carry signal wires well out of harms way were often substantial, sometimes carrying several signal wires. Indeed, there are instances of wires being cantilevered out from the main post. There was also at least one example of a complicated structure carrying a matrix of signal wires, all entering horizontally at different levels and leading to ground level vertically via pulleys positioned variously on the matrix. The whole was like a lattice between two posts - a most peculiar affair!

TABLE 9 - BUILDINGS and ASSOCIATED STRUCTURES

TABLE 9 - BUILDINGS and ASSOCIATED STRUCTURES	All periods	
MAIN WALLS - Station Buildings and other public facilities, including Signal Cabins. [1]	Burnt-sienna all over.	
MAIN WALLS - Locomotive, Goods Sheds and other operational buildings and structures, including Water Tank bases and Permanent Way Cabins. [1]	Virtually all creosoted - see text.	
DOORS, including semi-glazed and/or panelled doors, both external and internal.	Public facilities:	Usually purple-brown all over. Sometimes there were variations with burnt-sienna replacing purple-brown either all over or just on panels.
	Operational structures:	Burnt-sienna
WINDOWS, including frames and glazing bars (astragals).	Public facilities:	Purple-brown or white. Sometimes the frames were purple-brown and the bars white. (Refer to photographs if possible.)
	Operational structures:	Burnt-sienna throughout. Sometimes glazing bars were white.
PROJECTIONS, CORNER POSTS, FACINGS, DOOR FRAMES	Public facilities:	Purple-brown
	Operational structures:	Burnt-sienna
CANOPY COLUMNS	Purple-brown	
CANOPY BRACKETS	Burnt-sienna	
GUTTERING and DOWN PIPES	Purple-brown	
ROOFS (SLATE)	Left natural colour	
ROOFS (CORRUGATED IRON)	Red-oxide	
SIGNAL CABIN: ROOF RIDGE, FINIALS, STEPS, HANDRAILS	Purple-brown	
FENCING & SMALL GATES	Creosoted timber [2] (in earlier days at least some platform fencing was white)	
MAIN YARD GATES	White	
LEVEL CROSSING GATES	White Red diamond target, square lamp plate and lamp Black ironwork	
LAMP POSTS	Purple-brown (station name sometimes engraved in lamp glass)	
STATION and SIGNAL CABIN NAME BOARDS [3]	Cream background [3] Chocolate letters and beading [3] Posts and finials varied: white, burnt-sienna, two-tone, matched fencing.	
(I) Flush Style	See Plate 63 of Garve and Plate 65 of Tomatin.	
(II) Proud Style	Dark background with white border White letters individually set out proud of the backing. Posts and finials varied: as Flush Style. See Plate 68 of Altnabreac.	

TABLE 9 - BUILDINGS and ASSOCIATED STRUCTURES	All periods
PUBLICITY & TIMETABLE BOARDS	Bright red with black letters and mouldings, [4] with the legend: **The HIGHLAND RAILWAY** **Via DUNKELD**
TRESPASS and other WARNING BOARDS:	
Wooden post and backboard	Burnt-sienna
Wood (very early style) with hand-painted letters.	Not known: possibly white letters on dark background.

Plate 65 Station name board - flush style: Tomatin (1936). The overall height of each letter of the station name was 10 ½" with 2 ½" wide strokes. Note the height above sea level on the name board, each letter/number being 1 ½" high ¼" stroke. Note also the signal wire post carrying seven wires. Contrast the typeface with that of Garve in Plate 63.

[RAS Marketing - Photomatic 674

Plate 66. Lybster locomotive shed, apparently with a gloss paint finish, but more likely recently-applied creosote. Note the position of the two lamps on the cab, the front lamp with its four-legged carrying stand: and how prominent they all are.　　*[Real Photographs 44745*

TABLE 9 - BUILDINGS and ASSOCIATED STRUCTURES	All periods
Enamelled (pre-1912 style): 24" x 18" iron plate screwed to backboard.	(Light) chocolate letters on a white ground. [3]
Cast iron (post-1912 style): 25" x 16" TRESPASS and 16" x 12" BEWARE OF TRAINS plate bolted directly to post.	Raised block white letters on a black ground.
NORTH/SOUTH BOARDS: Wood 39" x 21"	(Light) chocolate letters on a white ground, varnished, thus: **PASSENGERS** *going* **NORTH** *keep* **THIS** *side*
STATION SEATS	Purple-brown with white lettering (station name on top rail)
BOARDING STOOLS	Purple-brown with white lettering (**H.R** on long sides)
BARROWS and HURLIES	Purple-brown with white lettering (tare weight and station name on side rails e.g. *1c. 2q. 19lb. Struan St"*)
STEELYARD and WEIGHBRIDGE HOUSINGS (those found both on station platforms and in goods yards)	Burnt-sienna Those in goods yards had felted roofs.
WATER TANKS (metal parts)	Purple-Brown border enclosing burnt-sienna panels.
TANK GAUGE	White board, black pointer, bars and figures.
"No water to be had at ... " BOARDS	Black with white letters
WATER COLUMNS:	
MAIN COLUMN	Burnt-sienna
OPERATING GEAR	Burnt-sienna or black
TOP CAP	Purple-brown
BASE	Purple-brown
INTEGRAL STOVE	Black

[1] Where the buildings were of wooden construction. Stonework was left in its natural state.

[2] It has been stated that fences were painted burnt-sienna: this seems highly unlikely.

[3] Cream has also been described as white and stone. Given that the these nameboards were enamelled iron, it is possible that the underlying colour was indeed white but the enamelling process gave a yellowish tinge.

Burnt-sienna has also been described as light chocolate, milk chocolate brown, and red brown. Again, perhaps the underlying colour has been affected by the enamelling process.

According to one source, in Highland days signal cabin nameboards were lettered " ..... CABIN" with the nameboard positioned on the front of the cabin. However, many photographs show otherwise. Confirmation of both naming conventions and positioning would be welcome: it would be interesting to know how DRUIMUACHDAR SUMMIT NORTH CABIN was handled!

[4] Some personal recollections have stated that these had black boards, red mouldings, and white letters. Photographs of Lybster, Dornoch and Fort George support this. It would appear that the red boards were of the type that had raised letters (possibly cast iron), and the black boards had painted letters.

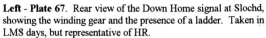

Left - Plate 67. Rear view of the Down Home signal at Slochd, showing the winding gear and the presence of a ladder. Taken in LMS days, but representative of HR.

[RAS Marketing - Ken Nunn 5544

Plate 68.   Station name board - proud style: Altnabreac - Up platform 7th October 1953.   *[James Stevenson*

Plate 69.   Blair-Atholl south end, showing a typical scene of signal, level crossing and signal cabin, including a lead-in signal wire post. The arriving train is a Down afternoon goods hauled by locomotive No. 119 *Loch Insh* which is in the process of giving up the tablet for the single section from Killiecrankie. An empty pouch will be taken up, in order to ensure that the locomotive always has a pouch on board. All such operations were exchanges, rather than one-way, to sustain this equilibrium. Although not particularly sharp, this shot has plenty of atmosphere.

[AG Ellis collection 38512

TABLE 10 - SIGNALLING and ALLIED APPARATUS

TABLE 10 - SIGNALLING and ALLIED APPARATUS	All periods	
SIGNAL POSTS	White, except for lower 3ft. which was usually red-oxide but sometimes burnt-sienna (as when on station platforms). But see Plate 64.	
FINIALS	White, but base and cone clamp (where fitted [1]) burnt-sienna.	
LADDERS	Black, except for lower 3ft. which was finished same as signal post.	
ARMS:	Front Face:	Rear Face:
HOME	Signal red, with white stripe only 4" wide 9" from end. See Plate 64.	White, with black stripe as front.
DISTANT	Signal red, with white fish-tail stripe 4" wide 9" in. See Plate 64.	White, with black fish-tail stripe as front.
SHUNT & SET BACK	Skeleton or bow-tie section signal red with white stripe at intersection; white "S".	White, with black "S".
MOUNTING PLATES and SPECTACLE FRAMES	White	
LAMPS and ALL IRONWORK	Black	
WINDLASS GEAR	Red-oxide	
SIGNAL WIRE POSTS	Commonly burnt-sienna but also white, especially on or near station platforms. Ironwork: Black. It is likely that some were simply creosoted, especially those some distance from stations.	
TABLET EXCHANGE APPARATUS	Main body: Burnt-sienna Counterweight: White Operating ironwork: Black	
FORK CUPBOARD	Burnt-sienna	
PLATFORM	Creosote	
LAMP POST	Burnt-sienna	
GROUND SIGNALS	Black, with round part of "stop" face red. "Clear" face showed white light.	
[1] Clamps were fitted on M&H finials.		

TABLE 11 - MISCELLANEOUS ITEMS

TABLE 11 - MISCELLANEOUS ITEMS	All periods
BRIDGES, OVER & UNDER LINE, TURNTABLES, etc.	Ironwork generally mid-grey, but certain bridges such as Clachnaharry swing bridge and the bridge over the River Tilt at Blair Atholl were white in order, it is said, to minimise problems with thermal expansion. It is thought that originally bridges were not numbered on the Highland Railway, being known by chainage (miles and chains, based on mileposts). But they were numbered at some stage, at least by the beginning of the twentieth century.
STATION FOOTBRIDGES	Officially purple-brown, some apparently very light in photos.
STATION PLATFORMS	Any timber: creosoted. Other materials left in natural state. Earlier styles had an ash/gravel surface with 12" timber edge. Ticket platforms were usually all-timber construction; often platform extensions would also be all timber. (Platform edges were *not* painted white.)
POINT LEVERS	Black with white counterweight
LINESIDE FENCING	Creosoted
STILES	Elaborate versions: Purple-brown Simple versions: Creosoted
TELEGRAPH POLES	Timber: Creosoted Ironwork: Black
SNOW FENCES	Normally creosoted, although repairs and extensions likely to be left in natural state.
SNOW / SAND BLOWERS	Creosoted
GRADIENT & MILEPOSTS	White, with chocolate brown numbers.
BUFFER STOPS	Black, with red baulk. Also red lamp on passenger roads.
PERMANENT WAY HUTS, BINS and BOTHIES	Creosoted all over. Corrugated iron roofs: Red-oxide.
HYDRAULIC CRANES ON KYLE PIER	Mid-grey ironwork with burnt-sienna cabin. Some carried white lifebelts with black lettering, hung on red board.
STEAMSHIPS (HR)	Not known. Only known photograph has one visible at Strome Ferry. All sold by 1882 (Kyle opened from 1897).
ROAD VEHICLES	Not used operationally. All off-line cartage done by contractors. However, the Highland did own three motor cars, but their livery is not known. One vehicle (DS 55) was used for advertising and was festooned appropriately - see Plate 242 in P Tatlow's *Highland Miscellany*.

CHAPTER 7 - LOCOMOTIVE CAST NUMBER PLATES AND NUMERALS

The various different styles were as follows, being generally applied to new locomotives built between the dates shown. The first date is the date of introduction; the second date is when the plates were superseded by a later design. Old style plates on locomotives were sometimes replaced by newer versions. Occasionally they were still applied to new locomotives despite being superseded, as described below.

STROUDLEY / JONES - 1865-1896

Figure 10 shows Stroudley's cast brass number plate style, which was not only applied retrospectively to Barclay locomotives, but which Jones continued to use - see Plate 70. The scroll-type numerals are shown in Figures 9, 10 and 11: these are reduced copies of Neilson's full size originals for the 'Strath' Class 4-4-0. Sharp Stewart drawings for the number plates for HR Nos. 103 to 117 (the 'Big Goods' Class 4-6-0) are to all intents and purposes identical, being proportionately smaller to enable the three digit number to fit the number plate - see Figures 12 and 13.

The last four 'Skye Bogie' Class 'L' 4-4-0s were completed during Peter Drummond's term of office, having been treated as stock jobs in Lochgorm Works, to be finished from mainly existing parts as required. Although Drummond made some alterations from the original Jones design, he used up sets of Stroudley/Jones style number plates as their original owners - old 2-4-0s - were withdrawn and scrapped.

These last four Skye Bogies were numbered 5 (32), 6 (33), 7 (34) and 48. The first three were renumbered as further old 2-4-0s were scrapped. No. 48 had the Stroudley/Jones style of plates from new in 1901, an older 2-4-0 No. 48 having been in use as a stationary boiler from 1894 until 1901.

DRUMMOND I - 1898-1904

Figures 14 and 15 show Drummond's flat-style number plate, the numerals being shown in Figure 16. The numeral "3" was round-topped if built by contractors (i.e. Nos. 3, 134, 143), yet the Lochgorm-built 'Scrap Tank' Class 0-6-0T No. 23 has a flat-topped "3" on the same style of plate.

DRUMMOND II - 1905 ON

Drummond changed to a different larger style with raised numerals and company name, a couple of years after the change to the all-over olive green livery, for no confirmed reason One possibility is that the new design was cheaper to make, in that there could be a single number plate master and separate and re-usable masters for each number, whereas the previous design required a different master each time. The first engine to carry Drummond's second style of number plate - 'Passenger Tank' Class 0-4-4T No. 25 - had the numerals rather crudely cast, the "5" being askew.

Figures 17, 18 and 19 show the style. All available evidence indicates that later on Cumming used the identical style on his locomotives. Specifications survive for the Cumming plates whereas there are only photographs for Drummond plates: hence the quoted source for the Drummond II drawings.

Plate 70. Jones cast brass number plate on 'Strath' Class 4-4-0 of 1892 No. 89 *Sir George*.　　　[HC Casserley 4263

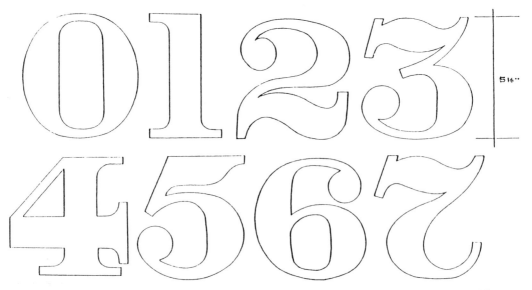

Figure 9. Stroudley / Jones numerals 0 - 7. Apparently the 9 was *not* an upside down 6. Two digit numbers were as drawn 5 ⅛" high x 4" wide. Single and triple digit numbers were made to fit the available space. The dimensions of single digit numbers are not known; a known triple digit example is given in Figure 11. Taken from Neilson & Co.'s works drawing 3282 for 'Strath' Class 4-4-0 Nos. 89-100 of 1892.

[Peter Tatlow collection

Figure 10. Stroudley / Jones number plate and numerals 8 - 9. Cast brass 17 ¼" x 11 ⅜". Company name and grooves engraved in flat polished rim and filled with black wax. Polished numerals raised from a yellow or blue (Stroudley) or vermilion (Jones) background. Taken from Neilson & Co.'s works drawing 3281 for 'Strath' Class 4-4-0 Nos. 89-100 of 1892. *[Peter Tatlow collection*

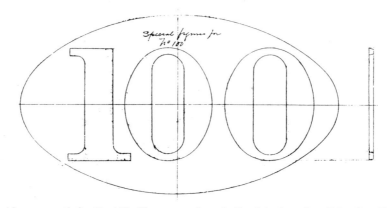

Figure 11. Stroudley / Jones numerals for No. 100. The zeros are "squashed" and the 1 smaller. Taken from Neilson & Co.'s works drawing 3282 for 'Strath' Class 4-4-0 Nos. 89-100 of 1892. *[Peter Tatlow collection*

Highland Railway Liveries

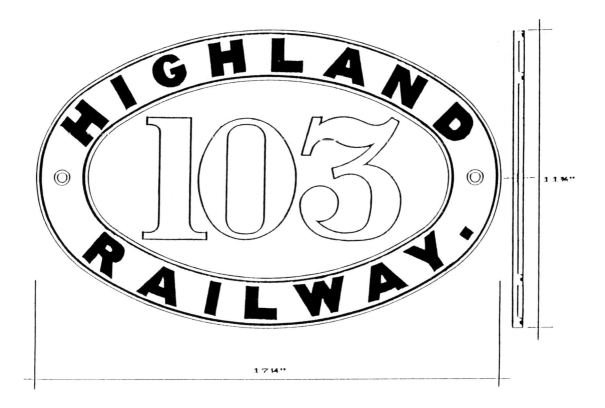

Figure 12. Jones number plate and numerals. Identical in size and style to previous version, namely 17 ¼" x 11 ⅜" overall, except that numerals for the triple digit numbers were of different proportions, i.e. 4 ⅝" high x 4" wide. Taken from Sharp Stewart works drawing 10061 for the 'Big Goods' Class 4-6-0 of 1894.   *[Eddie Bellass*

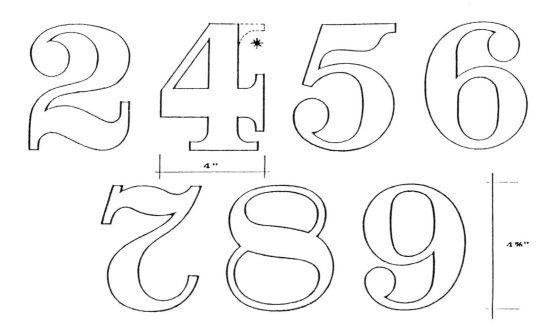

Figure 13. Jones numerals, 4 ⅝" high x 4" wide. Note that the "4" applied to Nos. 104/114 in 1894 had no top rear serif. Two years later, however, No. 124 *Loch Laggan* regained this serif. Taken from Sharp Stewart works drawing 10061 for the 'Big Goods' Class.

[Eddie Bellass

Figure 14. Drummond I flat style number plate. . Cast brass plate, 18" x 11", polished with grooves and characters engraved and filled with black wax. Taken from Dübs drawing 90079 for the 'Small Ben' Class 4-4-0 of 1898. *[Eddie Bellass*

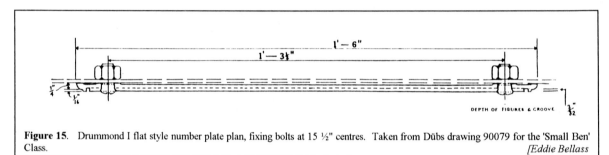

Figure 15. Drummond I flat style number plate plan, fixing bolts at 15 ½" centres. Taken from Dübs drawing 90079 for the 'Small Ben' Class. *[Eddie Bellass*

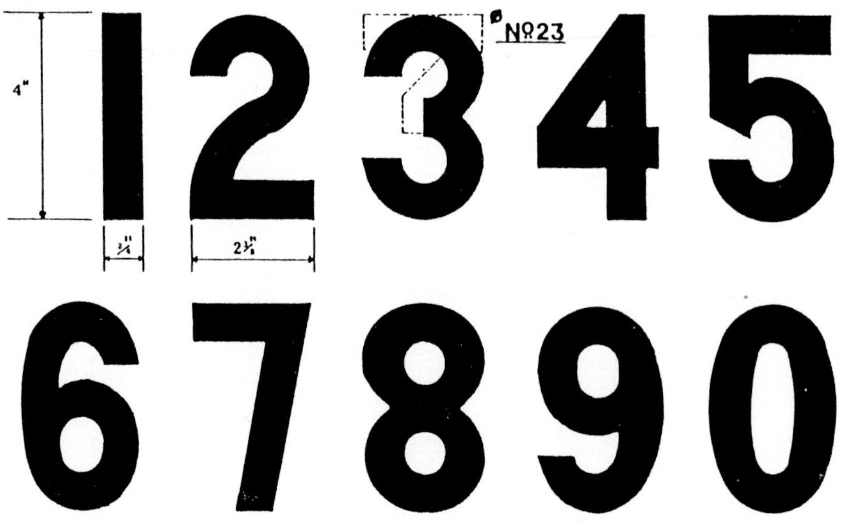

Figure 16. Drummond I flat style numerals, 4" high, mostly 2 ⅜" wide, although the "1" is only ¾" wide. Taken from Dübs drawing 90079 for the 'Small Ben' Class. *[Eddie Bellass*

Highland Railway Liveries

Figure 17. Drummond II / Cumming raised style number plate. Cast brass or gunmetal plate, 22 ½" x 15 ⅜", polished rims and characters raised from black background. Taken from Hawthorn Leslie drawing 114 for the 'Inverness Goods' Class 4-6-0 of 1918. *[Eddie Bellass*

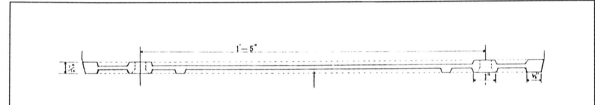

Figure 18. Drummond II / Cumming raised style number plate plan, fixing bolts at 17" centres, 1" below horizontal centre line. Taken from Hawthorn Leslie drawing 114 for the 'Inverness Goods' Class 4-6-0. *[Eddie Bellass*

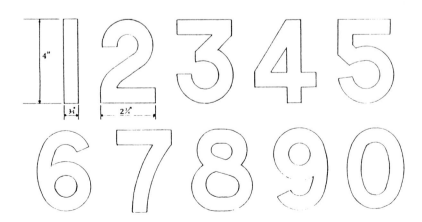

Figure 19. Drummond II / Cumming raised style numerals, still 4" high, slightly wider at 2 ¾" wide, although the "1" is still just ¾" wide. Taken from Hawthorn Leslie drawing 114 for the 'Inverness Goods' Class. *[Eddie Bellass*

The two 'Snaigow' Class superheated 4-4-0s of 1916 - Nos. 73 and 74 - had a hybrid style of number plate. The overall style was nominally that of Jones, that is to say, smaller than that of Drummond II, and the numerals were raised, scroll style. The company title was raised, in apparently serifed letters joined to the inner and outer rims, unlike any other kind of HR number plate - see Figure 22. Also worth noting is that No. 73 was delivered from the makers with a round-topped "3" painted on its front buffer beam (and possibly on the tender back). It was substituted with a straight-topped "3" by the HR at some later date. See Plate 71.

Cumming reverted to the Drummond II raised-style for later locomotives, using gunmetal instead of brass. Brass can be almost any copper/zinc alloy, whereas gunmetal is a specific bronze containing copper/tin/zinc in the ratio 88:10:2. Presumably, gunmetal was simply a more modern material. Cumming plates were sometimes retro-fitted to earlier locomotives - Plate 72 for example.

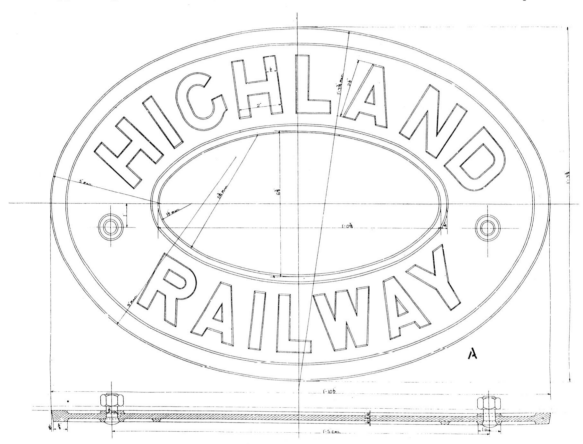

Figure 20. Cumming raised style number plate. Taken from R&W Hawthorn Leslie & Co. Ltd.'s works drawing 114 for 'Inverness Goods' Class 4-6-0 Nos. 75-78 of 1918. Understood to be the same as Drummond II style, differing only in the composition of the metal.

[Peter Tatlow collection

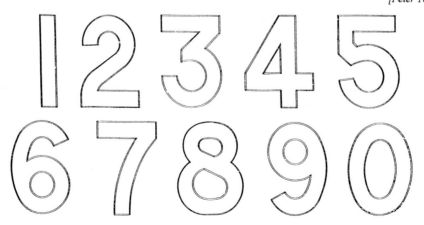

Figure 21. Cumming raised style numerals. Taken from R&W Hawthorn Leslie & Co. Ltd.'s works drawing 114 for 'Inverness Goods' Class 4-6-0 Nos. 75-78 of 1918.

[Peter Tatlow collection

Plate 71. 4-4-0 No. 73 *Snaigow*, showing Cumming's Stroudley style number plate. Although a dark photograph taken from a postcard, the number plate shows up well. Note also the position of the full-stop on the tender between the company initials.

[HRS collection - Locomotive Magazine Series 5243

DUPLICATE SUFFIXES

Any duplicate suffixes were usually painted on reportedly in white, and sometimes within the cast plate or else above it. The letter "A" was for duplicate engines in revenue service and the letter "B" for works and shed shunters, etc. A photograph shows that the suffix was on at least one occasion painted on the buffer beam beside the number. [16]

NUMBER PLATE POSITIONING

All number plates for tender locomotives were positioned on the cab side, although their height and precise position varied a little. Where the lining outlined the splasher, they were usually inside the splasher panel but sometimes higher up the cab side inside the cab side lining: this was the case with Small and Medium Goods Classes, where the splasher was too small to accommodate the number plate. Tank engines in general had theirs on the bunker behind the cab opening, even if there was precious little space - as with No. 118 *Gordon Castle*. However, the Lochgorm and Needlefield tanks had theirs on the side sheeting forward of the cab. The 'Yankee Tank' Class 4-4-0Ts had theirs on the tank side at first, well forward of the cab, although all but No. 101 later reverted to the bunker position. The number and works plates on No. 101 appeared in all three positions described above.

Plate 72. Cumming raised style number plate of preserved 'Big Goods' No. 103. *[Barry Eagles*

---

[16] Iain Sutherland, *The Wick and Lybster Light Railway*, published by the author, has a plate on page 39 of 0-4-4T No. 53[A] *Lybster* clearly with the superscript A.

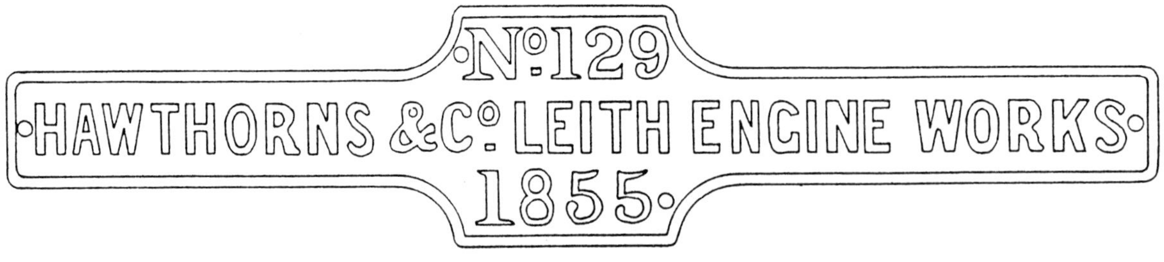

N.º 129

·HAWTHORNS &C.º LEITH ENGINE WORKS·

1855·

Figure 24. Hawthorn (Leith) works plate of I&NR No. 1 *Raigmore*. Cast brass, overall 31 5/16" x 3 ⅛", centre section 6 ¼" square at corners, characters and rim raised from background. Scale of drawing approx. 20% full size.

[Eddie Bellass, from plate No. 138 of 1856, courtesy Keith Buckle

The single Kitson: Kitson & Co. of Leeds supplied but one Highland locomotive, and that was Dunrobin ordered by the Duke Of Sutherland for his own railway, delivered in 1870 and bought by the Highland in 1895. Why Kitson was chosen is lost in the mists of time: it could be speculated that Leeds was relatively-speaking not far from the Duke's business interests in Stafford.

The Glasgow three: The history of the other manufacturers is inextricably intertwined. [18] The North British Locomotive Co. Ltd was formed in 1903 by the amalgamation of the three major locomotive builders in Glasgow: Sharp, Stewart &

Co. Ltd, Neilson, Reid & Co. and Dübs & Co., to counter the competition coming mainly from Baldwin's in the USA. The foundation of all these firms was Neilson & Co.

Walter Neilson, born 1819, started young at 17 as a partner in Mitchell & Neilson trading in Stobcross in Hydepark Street. The firm went through several name changes becoming Neilson & Co. around 1855. James Reid joined as works manager in 1851, leaving for Sharp, Stewart in Manchester in 1858. Henry Dübs succeeded Reid. Having outgrown the Hydepark Street premises, another works was built in Springburn in 1862. Called Hydepark Works, it

Figure 25. Early Neilson works plate of I&AJR No. 30 *Prince*. Cast brass, 14 ½" x 8 11/16", characters and rim raised from background. Scale of drawing approx. 20% full size.

[Eddie Bellass,
from original plate, courtesy Keith Buckle

Figure 26. Clyde Loco works plate of 'Clyde Bogie' Class No. 77 *Lovat*. Flat brass plate, 10 ¾" x 6 ¾", characters and grooves engraved and filled in black. Scale of drawing approx. 20% full size.

[Eddie Bellass,
from an enlargement of Plate 7

Plate 74. Showing the Dübs brick design that was the origin of the NBL plate. *[Howard Geddes collection*

Plate 75. Example of an NBL works plate (non-Highland). *[Barry Eagles*

---

[18] *The Springburn Story* by John Thomas, David & Charles 1974 provides a detailed account of the Springburn area in general. I have also referred to *A History of the North British Locomotive Co. Ltd*, published in 1953 by NBL and distributed free to selected businesses; this provides a succinct and definitive celebration of NBL and its predecessors.

Plate 71. 4-4-0 No. 73 *Snaigow*, showing Cumming's Stroudley style number plate. Although a dark photograph taken from a postcard, the number plate shows up well. Note also the position of the full-stop on the tender between the company initials.

[HRS collection - Locomotive Magazine Series 5243

DUPLICATE SUFFIXES

Any duplicate suffixes were usually painted on reportedly in white, and sometimes within the cast plate or else above it. The letter "A" was for duplicate engines in revenue service and the letter "B" for works and shed shunters, etc. A photograph shows that the suffix was on at least one occasion painted on the buffer beam beside the number. [16]

NUMBER PLATE POSITIONING

All number plates for tender locomotives were positioned on the cab side, although their height and precise position varied a little. Where the lining outlined the splasher, they were usually inside the splasher panel but sometimes higher up the cab side inside the cab side lining: this was the case with Small and Medium Goods Classes, where the splasher was too small to accommodate the number plate. Tank engines in general had theirs on the bunker behind the cab opening, even if there was precious little space - as with No. 118 *Gordon Castle*. However, the Lochgorm and Needlefield tanks had theirs on the side sheeting forward of the cab. The 'Yankee Tank' Class 4-4-0Ts had theirs on the tank side at first, well forward of the cab, although all but No. 101 later reverted to the bunker position. The number and works plates on No. 101 appeared in all three positions described above.

Plate 72. Cumming raised style number plate of preserved 'Big Goods' No. 103. *[Barry Eagles*

---

[16] Iain Sutherland, *The Wick and Lybster Light Railway*, published by the author, has a plate on page 39 of 0-4-4T No. 53[A] *Lybster* clearly with the superscript A.

Figure 22. (Conjectural) hybrid style exclusive to Cumming 4-4-0 Nos. 73 and 74. Material and dimensions are not known but are calculated to be as Jones' size: 17 ¼" x 11 ⅜". Outer rims and Company name in Jones' style, but raised rather than engraved. The numerals 7 and 3 are also unique to this class but the 4 closely resembles Jones' serifed 4. Calculated from Hawthorn Leslie cab erection drawings (which show outline of ellipse) and high quality builder's photographs. *[Eddie Bellass*

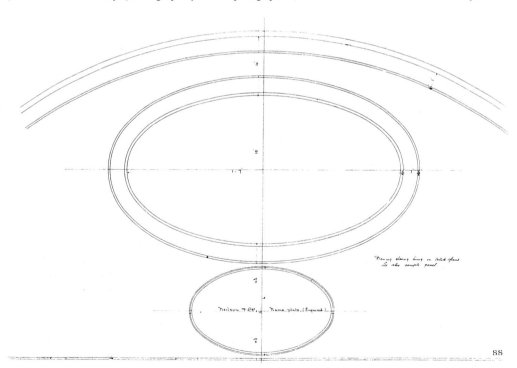

Figure 23. Lining arrangements for 'Strath' Class 4-4-0: splasher, footplate edge, number plate and works plate surrounds. Taken from Neilson & Co.'s works drawing 3569 of 14th April 1892. *[Peter Tatlow collection*

CHAPTER 8 - MANUFACTURERS' WORKS PLATES

The Highland Railway was supplied by a variety of manufacturers, as well as building their own stock at Lochgorm Works. Rolling stock was very much a product of the times and thus what we would call today hi-tech, i.e. of the most advanced design. Every manufacturer was desirous of publicising the fact that they had supplied the equipment. A works plate was the usual way of so doing, placed in a prominent yet discreet place. This chapter covers these works plates for locomotives, where there is a reasonable amount of information. The Lochgorm works plates of the Highland Railway Co. itself are included in Table 12.

Solebar plates for coaching stock and wagons are not covered. First, there were many more suppliers, and secondly information is currently much more scanty, which together take their detailed coverage well beyond the scope of this book.

THE MANUFACTURERS

Although not directly related to the Highland Railway Co., the story of the explosion of industrial activity in the 19th Century as it applied to the great locomotive manufacturers does reflect on the source of Highland locomotives. The following will help put this into perspective, especially as the story is quite convoluted. A brief history of the Highland's own Lochgorm Works is also given.

The two Hawthorns: Strangely, the first and last locomotives supplied were from Hawthorns. The very early locomotives were supplied by Hawthorn & Co., Leith; and the Cumming locomotives were supplied by R&W Hawthorn, Leslie & Co. Ltd, Newcastle. Hawthorns of Leith were an offshoot of

R&W Hawthorn & Co., Newcastle, set up by them to avoid having to ship locomotives by sea from Newcastle to Scotland. When the rail link was achieved with the opening of the Royal Border Bridge in 1850, the Leith company was sold and continued to build locomotives in its own right until the mid 1880s.

Hawthorn & Co. operated out of Leith Engine Works and supplied all the locomotives from the opening of the Inverness & Nairn in 1855 until shortly before the opening of the line to Perth - sixteen locomotives in total. Then, they lost the tender for the Small Goods and Glenbarry classes. However, there was a contractual agreement still in effect from 1859. This contract was fulfilled when they supplied the first two of the Glenbarry class. Neilsons supplied the other six of that first batch. Hawthorns then drop out of the picture.

R&W Hawthorn, Leslie & Co. Ltd, as is well known, supplied all the Cumming locomotives as well as the ill-fated River class. They operated from the Forth Banks Loco Works in Newcastle-on-Tyne. As R&W Hawthorn & Co., they were building locomotives in the 1830s, e.g. No. 43 *Sunbeam* for the Stockton & Darlington Rly., a pram-like 2-2-0T. [17] And, of course, they established Hawthorns in Leith.

It is not clear why Hawthorns of Newcastle should have got involved with the Highland when they did. One explanation is that they could provide a shorter lead-time than either Lochgorm or NBL. Whether this had anything to do with Frederick Smith's close Newcastle connections, one cannot say: probably not. Forth Banks closed in 1960.

Plate 73. Dübs works plate of 'Small Ben' Class No. 2 *Ben Alder*. *[Barry Eagles*

---

[17]   *Northern Echo Centenary Supplement* 1925 reproduced 1975 pp 42-3.

Figure 24. Hawthorn (Leith) works plate of I&NR No. 1 *Raigmore*. Cast brass, overall 31 5/16" x 3 ⅛", centre section 6 ¼" square at corners, characters and rim raised from background. Scale of drawing approx. 20% full size.

[Eddie Bellass, from plate No. 138 of 1856, courtesy Keith Buckle

The single Kitson: Kitson & Co. of Leeds supplied but one Highland locomotive, and that was Dunrobin ordered by the Duke Of Sutherland for his own railway, delivered in 1870 and bought by the Highland in 1895. Why Kitson was chosen is lost in the mists of time: it could be speculated that Leeds was relatively-speaking not far from the Duke's business interests in Stafford.

The Glasgow three: The history of the other manufacturers is inextricably intertwined. [18] The North British Locomotive Co. Ltd was formed in 1903 by the amalgamation of the three major locomotive builders in Glasgow: Sharp, Stewart &

Co. Ltd, Neilson, Reid & Co. and Dübs & Co., to counter the competition coming mainly from Baldwin's in the USA. The foundation of all these firms was Neilson & Co.

Walter Neilson, born 1819, started young at 17 as a partner in Mitchell & Neilson trading in Stobcross in Hydepark Street. The firm went through several name changes becoming Neilson & Co. around 1855. James Reid joined as works manager in 1851, leaving for Sharp, Stewart in Manchester in 1858. Henry Dübs succeeded Reid. Having outgrown the Hydepark Street premises, another works was built in Springburn in 1862. Called Hydepark Works, it

Figure 25. Early Neilson works plate of I&AJR No. 30 *Prince*. Cast brass, 14 ½" x 8 11/16", characters and rim raised from background. Scale of drawing approx. 20% full size.

[Eddie Bellass,
from original plate, courtesy Keith Buckle

Figure 26. Clyde Loco works plate of 'Clyde Bogie' Class No. 77 *Lovat*. Flat brass plate, 10 ¾" x 6 ¾", characters and grooves engraved and filled in black. Scale of drawing approx. 20% full size.

[Eddie Bellass,
from an enlargement of Plate 7

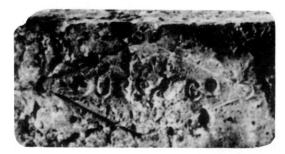

Plate 74. Showing the Dübs brick design that was the origin of the NBL plate.

[Howard Geddes collection

Plate 75. Example of an NBL works plate (non-Highland).

[Barry Eagles

[18] *The Springburn Story* by John Thomas, David & Charles 1974 provides a detailed account of the Springburn area in general. I have also referred to *A History of the North British Locomotive Co. Ltd*, published in 1953 by NBL and distributed free to selected businesses; this provides a succinct and definitive celebration of NBL and its predecessors.

Figure 27. Sharp, Stewart (Manchester) works plate, for 'Medium Goods' Class 2-4-0 No. 36 *Nairn*. Flat brass plate, 10" x 6 ¾", characters engraved and filled in black. Scale of drawing approx. one third full size. *[Eddie Bellass, based on plate No. 1501 for Furness Rly. 2-2-2T No. 22, courtesy Manchester Museum of Science & Industry*

Figure 28. Sharp, Stewart (Glasgow) works plate, for 'Big Goods' No. 103. Cast brass, 8" x 4 ¾", characters and rim raised from background. Scale of drawing approx. one third full size. *[Eddie Bellass, based on a rubbing of the original plate kindly supplied by Glasgow Transport Museum*

was built by Dübs. Dübs left in 1863, and James Reid returned to succeed him, this time as managing partner. Neilson withdrew from active management in 1872 and left entirely in 1876 after a disagreement with Reid, leaving Reid in sole charge. The firm was renamed Neilson, Reid & Co. in 1898, until the amalgamation of 1903. Reid's sons took over the running of the firm after Reid's death in 1894.

Henry Dübs left Neilsons to set up his own company in 1863: Dübs & Co. in Polmadie at Glasgow Locomotive Works. This firm remained the same and with the Dübs family still involved after Dübs' death in 1876 until 1903, when the works was renamed Queen's Park Works. The famous Dübs and NBL diamond nameplate originated with the logo on the bricks Dübs used to build his works, the clay for the bricks being the spoil of the site's excavation.

Undaunted by his enforced departure from his own business, Neilson set up the rival Clyde Locomotive Co. Ltd at the Clyde Locomotive Works in 1884 on the "other side of the [North British] tracks". The Highland, of course, had the very first locomotives from this firm - the Clyde Bogies. But, this outfit only lasted until 1888, when it was taken over by Sharp, Stewart. I have no record of Neilson's fate; approaching 70, he may have simply retired.

Sharp, Stewart of Manchester started out as Sharp, Roberts in 1822 with long antecedents in building and engineering. They expanded over the years, the family connections with Sharp, Stewart and Roberts literally dying out, the firm eventually outgrowing the Atlas Works in Manchester. Buyer met seller, and in 1888 they bought out the Clyde company, transferring operations to Glasgow, renaming themselves Sharp, Stewart & Co. Ltd and the works Atlas Works. And there they remained until 1903.

Plate 76. Example of a later style Neilson & Co. works plate (non-Highland). *[Barry Eagles*

Figure 29. Later style Neilson works plate of 'Strath' Class No. 100 *Glenbruar*. Flat brass plate, 9 ¾ x 5 ¾", characters engraved and filled in black. Scale of drawing approx. 30% full size. *[Eddie Bellass, from plate No. 3994 of 1889, courtesy Brian Hilton, and Neilson drawing No. 3569 (Figure 23), courtesy RB Constant*

Figure 30. Dübs works plate of 'Small Ben' Class No. 1 *Ben-y-Gloe*. Cast brass, 13 ¼" x 5 ⅜", characters and rim raised from background. Scale of drawing approx. 40% full size.

[Eddie Bellass,
from plate No. 3891 of 1900, courtesy Brian Hilton

Plate 77. Sharp, Stewart (Glasgow) works plate, for 'Big Goods' Class No. 104. Scale of plate approx. one half full size. *[Mary Casserley*

Figure 31. NBL works plate of 'Struan Banker' Class 0-6-4T No. 39. Cast brass, 13 ¼" x 5 ⅜", characters and rim raised from background. Scale of drawing approx. 40% full size.

[Eddie Bellass,
from plate No. 19057 of 1909, courtesy Brian Hilton

Plate 78. Example of a R&W Hawthorn, Leslie & Co. works plate (non-Highland). *[Barry Eagles*

Figure 32. R&W Hawthorn, Leslie & Co. works plate for No. 73 *Snaigow*. Cast brass or gunmetal plate, 9" x 6", characters and rims raised from background. Scale of drawing approx. one third full size. *[Eddie Bellass,*
based on plate No. 2791 of 1909, courtesy Brian Hilton

TABLE 12 - WORKS PLATE STYLE and USAGE

TABLE 12 - WORKS PLATE STYLE and USAGE	Period of application	Usage and Position [1]	
Hawthorn & Co. (Leith) - I Cast brass strip, 31 5/16" x 6 ¼" overall. Width of sidearms 3 ⅛". Centre section 6 ¼" square at corners. Characters and rim raised from background.	1855-1862	All classes	D
Hawthorn & Co. (Leith) - II Cast brass (?) oval, size not known.	1862-1863 [2]	All classes [3]	C
Neilson & Co. - I Cast brass strip, same dimensions and style as Hawthorn - I (?)	1859	Findhorn 0-4-0T[4]	D
Neilson & Co. - II Cast brass oval, 14 ½" x 8 11/16". Characters and rim raised from background.	1863	'Glenbarry' Class[3]	C
Neilson & Co. - III Cast brass oval, 9 ¾" x 5 ¾". Characters engraved and filled in black.	1892	'Strath' Class	D
Sharp, Stewart (Manchester) [5] Flat brass oval, 10" x 6 ¾". Characters engraved and filled in black.	1863-1864	'Small Goods' [3] 'Medium Goods' [3]	C C

Sharp, Stewart (Glasgow)
 	
Cast brass oval, 8" x 4 ¾".
Characters and rim raised from background.
	1894-1896	'Big Goods'
		'Dunrobin I'
		  rebuild
		'Dunrobin II'
			D
			Bunker
			  rear?
			C

Kitson & Co. Cast brass oval, size not known. Characters engraved and filled in black (?)	1870	'Dunrobin I'	D
Dübs & Co. Cast brass diamond, 13 ¼" x 5 ⅜". Characters and rim raised from background.	1874-1902	'Duke' 'Yankee Tank' 'Loch' 'Small Ben' 'Barney' 'Castle'	D B F D D (middle) S
Clyde Loco Co. Flat brass oval, 10 ¾" x 6 ¾". Characters and grooves engraved and filled in black.	1886	'Clyde Bogie'	D

TABLE 12 - WORKS PLATE STYLE and USAGE	Period of application	Usage and Position [1]	
North British Locomotive Co. ("The Combine") Cast brass diamond, 13 ¼" x 5 ⅜". Characters and rim raised from background.	1906-1917	'Small Ben' 'Barney' 'Castle' 'Big Ben' 'Struan Banker'	D D (middle) S D D
R&W Hawthorn, Leslie & Co. Cast brass (possibly gunmetal) oval, 9" x 6". Characters and rims raised from background.	1915-1921	All classes	Sl
Lochgorm I: Jones style Cast brass oval, 8" x 4". Characters and groove engraved and filled in black.	1869-1901	'Lochgorm Tank' 'Duke' 'Jones Tank' 'Skye Bogie' 'Strathpeffer'	Cr D Dm D Br
Lochgorm II: Drummond style Cast brass oval, 8" x 4". Characters and grooves engraved and filled in black.	1899-1906	'Small Ben' 'Scrap Tank' 'Passenger Tank'	D D D

[1]
D: in line with a driving wheel, either on footplate or wheel or coupling rod splasher.
Dm: in between drivers, on footplate valance.
C: on cab-side. Note that Lochgorm rebuilds sometimes resulted in a Lochgorm plate in the "D" position. [3]
Cr: in middle of cab-sheet, which extended forward.
B: on bunker-side.
Br: on bunker-rear when built; when rebuilt, on front sandbox.
F: on frame above footplate above rear bogie axle.
S: on smokebox, centre-line usually, sometimes on the smokebox saddle. When new smokeboxes were put on, the plate was sometimes moved to the middle of the driving wheel splasher. When first delivered, early 'Castles' had their Dübs plates on the raised portion of the mainframes enclosing the smokebox base. Some seem to have migrated upwards to the smokebox centre-line, e.g. No. 143 *Gordon Castle*. The 1913 and 1917 batches were delivered with works plates mounted on the smokebox centre-line.
Sl: on smokebox, slightly below centre line, in line with the smokebox door lower hinge.

[2]
A drawing of 0-4-0T No. 17 *Hopeman* as built in 5/1863 shows it with an oval works plate (see P Tatlow's *Highland Locomotives* Figure 15). No. 11 supplied in 10/1859 is confirmed having the strip style - see Plate 1. This leaves doubts whether Nos. 12-15 supplied between May and October 1862 and the first two 'Glenbarry's supplied later in 1863 had Strip or Oval style works plates. No photographic evidence has been found one way or the other: maybe the drawing is speculative.

[3]
Several photographs of these classes, in both as built and rebuilt conditions, have the engines without a visible works plate. It may be conjectured that the plates were originally on the cab-side (as evidenced by Figures 15 and 16 in P Tatlow's *Highland Locomotives*), and when Stroudley either applied his number plates, altered the cab or rebuilt them the original works plates were moved, perhaps to the tender/bunker rear but more likely to the inside of the frames. A replacement Lochgorm I works plate was only sometimes applied, according to photographs.

[4]
The 1859 Findhorn 0-4-0T was a standard Neilson product, called the Neilson Patent Shunter. One such, of 1862 vintage, is illustrated on page 19 of *The Springburn Story* by John Thomas, the original photograph being in the Mitchell Library. It is almost identical to No. 16, and shows the Neilson works plate more clearly than extant photographs of the Findhorn engine. It is very similar indeed to the pre-1863 Hawthorns of Leith works plate.

[5]
No photograph has been found showing a Highland engine with a Sharp, Stewart (Manchester) works plate.

The three firms amalgamated in the autumn of 1903, with William Lorimer ex-Dübs & Co. as Chairman. The new firm was known ever after as "the Combine". The Chief Managing Director was Hugh Reid (James Reid's son), who was no relation of his peer William Paton Reid, the Locomotive Superintendent of the North British Railway Co., only 800 yards away at Cowlairs.

Following the amalgamation, all orders for Highland locomotives placed with the new North British Locomotive Co. were completed at the former Dübs factory at Queen's Park Works, Polmadie.

Others: No other manufacturer supplied locomotives, although others did heavy repairs and did (unsuccessfully) tender.

LOCHGORM WORKS

From its opening in 1855, the Inverness & Nairn Railway had its maintenance facilities on the site of Loch Gorm, just to the north of the station approach at Inverness. These included locomotive running sheds, maintenance workshops and carriage sidings. Over the winter of 1862-63, and ready in time for the opening of the direct line to Perth, the Inverness & Aberdeen Junction Railway built a new locomotive running shed on the south side of the tracks. Designed by Joseph Mitchell, this was the famous roundhouse. The running shed was quite separate from Lochgorm Works.

Subsequently, carriage and wagons shops were erected on a piece of land known as Needlefield, just north of the Rose Street curve, and the relevant activities transferred to them. Although physically separate from the original works buildings, these shops were still reckoned to be part of the establishment known as Lochgorm Works. This left the original site concentrating almost exclusively on locomotive work, primarily on repairs with some new build.

Lochgorm Works as a whole covered 18 acres, with a two-road erecting shop capable of dealing with fourteen locomotives, plus all other shops, stores and other facilities needed to support the entire system. Stroudley initially organised the works into a thoroughly efficient operation; and in his time, Drummond reorganised the works, bringing it into the twentieth century. The first locomotive to be built at Lochgorm was Stroudley's 0-6-0T No. 56 *Balnain* in 1869, the last being Drummond's 0-4-4T No. 46 in 1906. In all, Lochgorm built 42 locomotives.

The works remained until 1959, although the erecting shop continues in use as a diesel maintenance depot.

Figure 33. Lochgorm works plate I: Jones style. Engraved brass, approx. 8" x 4". Scale of drawing ⅜ full size.
[Peter Tatlow

Plate 79. Lochgorm works plate I: Jones style.
[Mary Casserley

Plate 80. Lochgorm works plate II: Drummond style.
[Mary Casserley

Figure 34. Lochgorm works plate II: Drummond style. Engraved brass, approx. 8" x 4". Scale of drawing ⅜ full size.
[Peter Tatlow

Figure 35. BR replacement works plate for 'Passenger Tank' No. 55051. Cast iron, 8 7/16" x 4 ⅜". Scale of drawing approx. one third full size. *[Eddie Bellass, from original plate on ex-HR No. 25 Strathpeffer, courtesy Keith Buckle*

Plate 81. The BR works plate replaced the original Lochgorm II style plate which was removed from No. 55051 in 1952. Note the crudeness of the casting.

[Eddie Bellass collection - photo taken 10th September 1953

Plate 82. Lochgorm works plate II: Drummond style, on 'Small Ben' No. 14408 (ex-12) *Ben Hope*. *[HC Casserley 13827*

Plate 83. LMS replacement works plate on 'Small Ben' No. 14409 (ex-13) *Ben Alisky*. Contrast with Plate 82, both taken on 18th June 1937. *[HC Casserley 13829*

Plate 84. Another contrast with Plate 82. This time, note the difference in the LMS early serifed style of **BEN HOPE** and the later block style of **BEN HOPE**. *[HC Casserley 17091*

Plate 85. Jones Type E 8 ton open wagon No. 1003, built to Diagram 15, clearly showing the number plate. Note the builder's plate on the solebar on the left, which reads: **HIGHLAND RAILWAY LOCHGORM 1887 WORKS INVERNESS**. The photograph has been taken in Drummond's time, to demonstrate the cam-style of brake gear. Although braked on only one wheel, the brake could be operated from either side of the wagon. In Jones' time, there would have been no **H R** lettering. *[Neil Hunter collection*

CHAPTER 9 - LAMP CODES

This Chapter covers the Highland Railway's way of identifying the presence of trains and engines by means of lamps and other devices.

In contrast to most if not all other railways, the Highland did not use lamps, discs or banners to identify different types of train or their route. Fundamentally, the Highland used lamps and other devices solely to indicate the physical presence of a train, a whole train, and nothing but a train. Obviously, the presence of the train itself is shown, but sometimes the presence of *another* train was also indicated, as with "Engine Following" and "Train Divided" arrangements.

All traffic movements, whether of light engines or of trains, were identified in very much the same way. These arrangements evolved over time. The mature arrangements, as well as those in effect in more formative days according to the 1888 Rule Book, are described below One fact that as far as is known held constant is all lamps were painted bright red.

Curiously, the 1888 Rule Book states what lights (not lamps) must be displayed after sunset and during foggy or snowy weather, but often does not state what the arrangements are at other times. Indeed, 1888 Rule 261 states that lamps *must* be extinguished at daylight. Wording of the relevant rules strongly implies that generally lamps (lit or unlit) were not needed at all in clear weather during daylight. This inference is given further credence by the fact that the lights only identified the presence of a train, not its type: hence, there is no operational need to display even unlit lamps by day, since the train itself is perfectly visible.

This may also explain why contemporary photographs (necessarily taken in good conditions) often show engines without the proper complement of lamps. Main line trains tended to have correct lamps for two reasons: first, some of the journey could well have been in darkness, and secondly, the most convenient place to stow an unlit lamp would have been in its normal position. However, branch line and local trains and pilot engines appear to have been more variable.

Obviously, locomotives on shed, where many photographs were taken, could appear in any state.

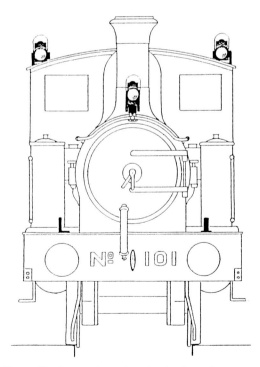

Figure 36. Lamp codes: tank engines hauling trains, except:
*   'Lochgorm' Class 0-6-0Ts: no lamp iron on right-hand side of cab roof
*   Drummond 'Struan Banker' Class 0-6-4Ts: lamp iron on right-hand side of bunker panel.

[Eddie Bellass

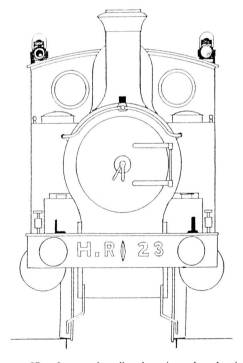

Figure 37. Lamp codes: all tank engines when shunting, exceptions as Figure 36.   *[Eddie Bellass*

Hence, for those modelling the Highland, best advice is that if lamps are to be included on a locomotive, a clear light should be shown, not a coloured one, whether head or tail. Further, a complete absence of lamps can be justified!

Finally, the authors are not aware of any photographs showing the Train Divided lamps in use, nor the various boards and lamps in use at the rear of a train.

Train Lamps: All train engines, irrespective of classification and including light engines, carried three lamps on every occasion that lights were required, namely after sunset, or during foggy or snowy weather. The lamps were:-

1. at the base of the chimney;
2. on the left-hand side (looking forward) of the cab, either on the roof or side-sheet;
3. on the right-hand side sheet of either the tender or the cab (or cab roof, if a tank engine).

The first showed a white light. Both the latter showed a red light to the rear as well as white to the front.

The train also carried a tail lamp, day or night. When required to be lit, it showed red to the rear. In earlier days, when lights were required the last

vehicle of the train had to carry an additional two side lamps, both showing white to the front and red to the rear: but during the day when lights were not required, instead of the (unlit) tail lamp, there had to be a board with the word LAST prominently displayed. This was called simply the Last Board. In no case is there ever a distinction made between passenger, goods or mixed trains.

If the train were double-headed, each engine had to have its own full complement of lamps, notably each had a head lamp.

The arrangements when there were banking engines are not clear. Since the rules are open to interpretation and it is known that other rules involving banking engines were regularly honoured in their breach (like buffering-up only when the train is stationary), it may be safely assumed that there were "interesting" variations, including having tail lamps on both rear vehicle and banker.

Light Engine Lamps: Light engines travelling bunker or tender first still had the three lamps in the right configuration, with the first lamp on the rear of the tender or bunker, top middle.

Latterly, it appears that light engines did not have to carry a tail lamp at all. Presumably it was deemed that the red-showing side lamps were sufficient warning. However, at least in 1888, they had had to

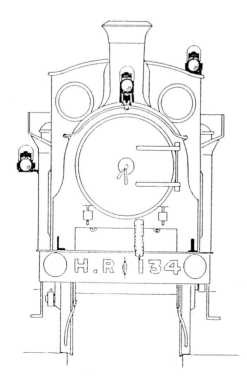

Figure 38. Lamp codes: all tender locomotives except Cumming's Classes.   [Eddie Bellass

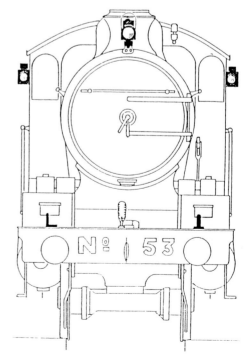

Figure 39. Lamp codes: all Cumming's Classes.

[Eddie Bellass

Plate 86. It has appeared several times in other places, but little excuse is needed to include this picture again here, showing off at Inverness Stroudley's second design of the large snowplough. Note the extended lamp iron on the snow plough. Snow and snowploughs have been extensively covered in a superbly illustrated two-part article by Niall Ferguson in the British Railway Journal, Nos. 49/50. It has been stated that the front engine is in Improved Engine Green, but the current feeling is that it is in fact in photographic grey: the finish is flat whilst the other locos are clearly glossy. *[David Jenkinson collection*

carry a red tail lamp *at all times*, although it need not be lit by day.

If more than one light engine were coupled together, each had to have its two side lamps and head lamp, but only one tail lamp was needed.

Shunting Lamps: There is no mention of shunting engines in the 1888 Rule Book. But later on, according to a modification to the 1907 Rule Book, shunting engines carried:-

"a Red Head Light (showing a White Light to the rear), and a Red Tail Light (showing a White Light to the front). The Head Light must be fixed on the right side and the Tail Light on the left side of the engine cab."

Note therefore that shunting engines did not require a head lamp on the smokebox nor a tail lamp on the bunker.

Engine Following Lamps: Where a special train or engine was to follow closely a previous train or a train was run in more than one portion, the preceding train or trains would normally display Boards, front and rear. That at the front was called a Red Board and was an oval with the legend ENGINE FOLLOWING intended to be fitted to the lamp iron over the left-hand buffer, whilst that at the rear was

called a Red Disc with the words UP on one side and DOWN on the other. [19]

Latterly (apparently after 1907), the Red Disc was superseded by the Red Board, it becoming known as the Engine Following Board.

Green lights replaced these Boards at night, in foggy weather, or in falling snow, both on the engine and the last vehicle. These green head and tail lights were carried in addition to the normal head and tail lamps.

Train Divided Lamps: At least in 1888, if a train had to be divided for any reason, two red lights had to be displayed on the front of the engine, indicating that part of the train had been left behind in section. These red lights were presumably in addition to all the other lamps and boards, and probably had to be displayed day or night.

Vehicle Protection Lamps: Lastly, it may be mentioned that employees working in or on stationary vehicles were afforded protection by means of a red light by night or a red flag by day, fixed to a lamp iron, that furthest from any parallel running line if needs be. Each end of the stationary line of vehicles might have to be protected in this way.

Similarly, because certain buffer stops, commonly

---

[19]   Plate 197 in P Tatlow's *Highland Miscellany* shows the Engine Following Board preserved in the National Railway Museum, whilst details of the rectangular Up/Down Board are in *Highland Railway Journal Nos. 31* and *32*.

those protecting the ends of running lines used by passenger trains, carried red lamps, any vehicles standing on those lines had present a red light to approaching trains.

Lamp Iron arrangements: In order to comply with the above regulations, most engines would need five lamp-irons as follows:-

- at the base of the chimney
- on the nearside front buffer beam
- on the nearside cab roof or side-sheet
- on the offside cab roof or bunker side (tank engines)
- on the offside cab side-sheet ('River' Class and Cumming's engines)
- on the offside tender side (other tender engines)
- at the top-middle of the bunker/tender

The first and last were sockets rather than the more familiar vertical strips. [20]

It seems that spare or unlit lamps were carried on the offside front buffer beam and the nearside rear buffer beam, both irons being set side-on. To attain symmetry and to handle the unlikely situation where a train engine would be both running in reverse and requiring an Engine Following Board or Lamp, it is likely that a lamp-iron would be provided on the offside rear buffer beam: this might also be the site

of a tail lamp when it was decreed for light engines. Thus, engines might be provided with eight lamp irons.

However, the early 2-4-0 tender locomotives seemed to manage without any buffer beam lamp irons until the 1890s. This is not surprising, given the lamp irons' normal usage, but does not square with the exceptional Train Divided and Engine Following rules. Further, many early tenders had no top-middle lamp sockets - probably a reflection that at that time tender engines were very much discouraged from travelling tender first hauling a train. Jones tenders had one nearside buffer beam lamp iron; Drummond tenders had them on both sides.

The three Cumming Classes (and, by the way, the first two 'Rivers' actually delivered to the Highland) had built-in lamp housings on both sides of the cab, instead of on the cab-roof / tender-side as "required" by the rules.

The one position missing from all this is the middle of the buffer beam, front and rear.

However, these is quite a loose linkage between lamp irons provided and the rules. When some of the exceptional configurations were demanded, the relevant lamps or boards were probably hung in any convenient place, if they were deployed at all.

Plate 87. Lochgorm works plate on rear bunker of 'Jones Tank' Class 4-4-0T No. 15010, where the number ought to have been in Highland days. Taken on 19th July 1931 at Inverness, it also shows the bunker lamp-iron arrangement, having been adapted from the original socket-style which would house the lamp's spike, to the more familiar lamp-iron style. *[HC Casserley 7720*

---

[20] The peculiar design of the head lamps specifically to fit the socket is discussed by Eddie Bellass in *Highland Railway Journal No. 31*, which includes drawings. These lamps were not free-standing, needing a four-legged stand which sometimes remained attached to the lamp when in use on the locomotive - see Plate 66. Side lamps were of a different design, with two bulls-eyes and two slots. The two designs were not interchangeable. There must have been at least one other more conventional design with a single bulls-eye and rear slot, but no details are known.

CHAPTER 10 - LMS AND BR LIVERIES

The appearance of the Highland Railway did not change overnight at grouping, when it became from 1st January 1923 a constituent of the London Midland and Scottish Railway. It took a little while for the new company to decide upon the liveries it would adopt and, once settled, these were only applied as repainting was required or new plant introduced. For instance locomotives and rolling stock were overhauled at the workshops at intervals usually determined by mileage run or a prescribed period of time. Examples of engines could be found still wearing the remnants of Highland livery in 1928 and wagons as late as 1938.

Some rolling stock and much line-side equipment survived to become part of the nationalised British Railways on 1st January 1948.

In the following paragraphs the manner in which LMS and British Railways liveries were applied to Highland equipment is discussed.

LOCOMOTIVES

The subject of the livery of LMS locomotives has been thoroughly documented by Bob Essery and David Jenkinson - see the bibliography. Detailed variations in the liveries carried by ex-HR engines are further explored in the RCTS books on Highland locomotives.

LMS Renumbering

Locomotives of the Northern Division of the LMS were renumbered by class into the following groups:

14xxx	Passenger tender engines
15xxx	Passenger tank engines
16xxx	Freight tank engines
17xxx	Freight tender engines

Within groups the numbers were organised by wheel arrangement, power classification in ascending order and date of introduction of the class. Many HR engines fell within the first two groups of numbers for tender and tank passenger classes, perhaps because there were few classes principally designed for use on freight workings. Even so, of these the Big Goods, Barney and Superheated Goods were from time to time rostered to work or assist passenger trains during the busy summer period.

LMS Livery

Prior to 1928, all classes of Highland locomotives of passenger description received the crimson lake livery - see Plate 25 for an application of the style. From 1928, with the introduction of the lined black livery for intermediate classes, all Highland locomotives surviving to receive a repaint were to have black applied in one form or another.

Plate 88. No. 14682 *Beaufort Castle*, showing the pre-1928 lined red LMS passenger livery, with the name in a straight line between the splashers.

[Real Photographs 44718

During the period of transition between the pre-1928 and post-1927 liveries, several engines appeared in hybrid styles. Some had been painted in the crimson lake livery, but transfers for the large tender numerals and for the cab side coat of arms were evidently not available. Photographs of the period show four 'Castle' Class 4-6-0s Nos. 14676, 14680, 14682 and 14693 and one 'Small Ben' Class 4-4-0 No. 14416 painted in red livery yet without numbers on the tenders. In addition, one if not two actually had LMS (probably hand painted) on the tender sides in conformity to the post-1927 crimson lake livery, by then reserved for the top link express engines. On the other hand, a few engines were painted black with numbers on the tender and coat of arms on the cab sides.

At the beginning of the post-1927 era, several freight engines seem to have had the intermediate livery's vermilion lining (or more likely pale yellow) applied, although not entitled to it.

From prior to World War II and until nationalisation on 1st January 1948, most engines, if they were repainted at all, received an unlined plain black livery.

Smokebox number plates were applied to engines repainted in the pre-1928 style, but on the whole were removed during visits to the paint shops subsequent to 1928.

Names

In most cases the LMS continued to apply names to those engines which had carried them at the time of grouping. The position and arrangement was generally as before (see Plate 25), except in the case of the' Castle' Class where the name was now arranged in a straight line across the wheel splasher: see Plate 88. The position of the name *Loch Garry* on No. 14387 was misplaced with the centre of the arc forward of the leading driving wheel centre, whilst No. 14392 *Loch Naver* was straight across the splasher (in 1928).

Up until 1928, the 4 inch high lettering was in gold serif style, shaded black to the lower right. From 1928 the serif style was generally continued, but the shading was omitted - see Plates 82 and 83. Whereas prior to 1936, the use of block style lettering was rare, from this date on it became the usual practice as engines were repainted; it was applied in pale yellow. [21] Contrast the serif and block styles applied to *Ben Hope* in Plates 82 and 84; note also the subtle flare to the block letters. However, one or two examples of block lettering had appeared from an early date. Known examples were: Nos. 14678 ('30) and 14688 (7/26). [22]

Misspelling of names occurred in a few cases, no doubt when, under LMS management, engines were put through foreign works rather than Lochgorm.

Plate 89. No. 14769 *Clan Cameron*, built in 1921 by Hawthorn Leslie, is seen at Perth in April 1929 in the post-1927 black livery fully lined in vermilion, or possibly pale yellow, for intermediate classes. The name *Clan Cameron* is applied in serif style letters in a straight line along the valance casing. The 4P power classification is placed just below the horizontal grab rail on the cab side. The engine is still fitted with Westinghouse brake gear, original builders' plate on the smoke box side and number plate mounted high on the smoke box door.

[AG Ellis collection 36014

---

[21]   For example: No. 14416 *Ben-a-Bhuird* - see Figure 8 in Cormack and Stevenson's *RCTS Highland Locomotives Book 2*.
[22]   Plate 105 Tatlow's *Highland Railway Locos* and Figure 37 in Cormack and Stevenson's *RCTS Highland Locomotives Book 2*.

Plate 90. 'Inverness Goods' Class 4-6-0 No. 17950, showing the pre-1928 black LMS goods livery.   *[David Jenkinson collection*

Those identified are listed in the table below.

No.	Incorrect Name	Correct Name [1]
14393	*Loch Laochal*	*Loch Laoghal*
14397	*Ben y-Gloe* then *Ben y'Gloe*	*Ben-y-Gloe*
14416	*Ben-a-Bhuird*	*Ben a'Bhuird*
14417	*Ben na Caillach*	*Ben na Caillich*
14421	*Ben Bhreac' Mhor*	*Ben Bhreac Mhor*
14422	*Ben Achaoruinn*	*Ben a'Chaoruinn*

[1]   As the Highland Railway Co. spelt them, not necessarily the spelling generally accepted in other spheres, e.g. *Ben a' Ghlo* is better than *Ben-y-Gloe*.

Power Classification

The LMS followed Midland Railway practice by introducing power classifications to all locomotives. This consisted of a number from 1 to 7 or unclassified, and a letter P or F to indicate passenger and freight respectively.

Until 1928 just the numeral was indicated on the cab-side of passenger classes only.

From 1928 all types of engine carried the power classification on the cab-side with the addition of the P or F. It was intended that the letter should follow the number, but there were occasional instances of ex-Highland engines having them reversed. The

following have been identified: Nos. 14522 ('29), 14759 (5/28) and 14762 ('28).

Builders' Plates

The LMS often removed the original builders' plates and replaced them with a small elliptical design of their own - thus achieving the anomaly of the LMS apparently stating they had built locomotives many years before the company existed. See Plate 83. A less ambiguous example was the plate on 'Small Ben' No. 14416 (ex-47) *Ben-a-Bhuird* which states "LMS built 1906 NB Loco".[23] Another, of 'Small Ben' No. 14406 (ex-10) *Ben Slioch*, announces "LMS rebuilt 1927 Kilmarnock".[24]

British Railways Renumbering and Livery

BR's renumbering scheme in the case of ex-LMS engines consisted of adding 40000 to their previous numbers. In this way, surviving Highland engines now started with 5 instead of 1.

Not many ex-Highland engines went through the shops for a full overhaul and repaint following nationalisation. Those to receive the early livery with **BRITISH RAILWAYS** across the tender or tank sides were: Nos. 55051, 55053, 57695, 57697, 57698 and 57955 - see Plate 91. However, two 'Small Bens' Nos. 54398 and 54399 had their numbers and names applied in Gill Sans according to the BR specification, but no lettering or totem on the tender sides. No. 57950 had the number in Gill

---

[23]   See Figure 8 in Cormack and Stevenson's *RCTS Highland Locomotives Book 2.*
[24]   See Figure 7 in Cormack and Stevenson's *RCTS Highland Locomotives Book 2.*

Plate 91. Drummond 'Passenger Tank' Class No. 55051 (ex-25 *Strathpeffer*), showing early British Railways livery. Outside St. Rollox shed, April 1949. *[RM Casserley collection*

Sans and a smokebox number applied, yet the tender remained untouched with "LMS" still visible.

No. 57955 later received the small BR totem. On the occasion of its second repaint under the auspices of BR, the Drummond 'Passenger Tank' No. 55053 received lined black livery for mixed traffic locomotives with the totem of the small lion astride a wheel - see Plate 92.

COACHES

The liveries of LMS coaches have also been fully specified - see the bibliography.

LMS Livery

From 1923, all repainted coaches would have received the crimson lake livery and up to 1934 would have been fully lined out around the panels above the waist line and around the lower portion at the ends and along the foot of the body sides, with the raised beading black edged with gold on gangwayed stock and pale yellow on non-gangwayed stock. See Plate 93.

From 1934, the lining was simplified to horizontal lines of two plain yellow lines between the cantrail and above the tops of the windows, together with a black line edged with yellow below the windows.

Former Highland carriages tended to retain their livery. An example was the spare set, all HR vehicles, which was stabled in the carriage shed at Aviemore and was brought out for events like the Elgin Highland Games. This lasted until the start of World War II at least in full LMS lined livery.

LMS Renumbering

Initially the LMS renumbered coaching stock by taking the existing numbers of the constituent company and placing them in a group in the same order. In the case of the HR, and many other companies, separate series of numbers had been used for each type of coach.

Highland passenger coaching stock was to be found in the following sequential ranges:

Type	First LMS Nos.
First	18591 to 18615
Composite	18616 to 18693
Third	18694 to 18847
Brake Third	18848 to 18864

From 1933, the LMS implemented a renumbering scheme to bring each type of coaching vehicle, of whatever origin, into a group of numbers, starting with the youngest vehicle with the highest number in the allotted group and numbering backwards. Highland stock was renumbered in ranges as shown in the table overleaf.

Some carriages had been down graded from composites to all thirds prior to the introduction of the renumbering scheme and therefore were to be found in the series for the lower grade. Others were similarly reclassified after the introduction of the scheme and as a result had to be renumbered again.

The second series of numbers can be distinguished by the use of block style numerals, as opposed to the serif style of the first series.

Plate 92. Drummond 'Passenger Tank' No. 55053 at The Mound on 2nd September 1955, showing later British Railways livery of lined black and the lion totem. *[Jack Templeton - Peter Tatlow collection*

Type	Second LMS Nos.
Special Saloon	823, 972 to 974
Corridor Third	3385 to 3399
Corridor Composite	4987 to 4999
Corridor Brake Third	6598 to 6599
Corridor Composite Brake	7398 to 7399
Semi-corridor Brake	18598 to 18599
Non-corr Lav Third	18965 to 18999
Non-corr Lav Comp	19966 to 19993
Non-corr Lav Third Brake	25696 to 25699
6-wheel Lav First	27401
6-wheel Composite	27233 to 27236
6-wheel Third	26911 to 26955

British Railways Renumbering and Livery

British Railways continued to use the same number with initially the prefix letter M to indicate its LMS origin. Later this was made the suffix and SC added as the prefix to indicate the region responsible for the maintenance and operation of the coach.

Most ex-HR coaches appear to have been painted carmine or remained crimson lake until withdrawn. But at least one ex-HR corridor coach received the British Railways livery of carmine below the waist and cream above. The known example was No. SC4993M.

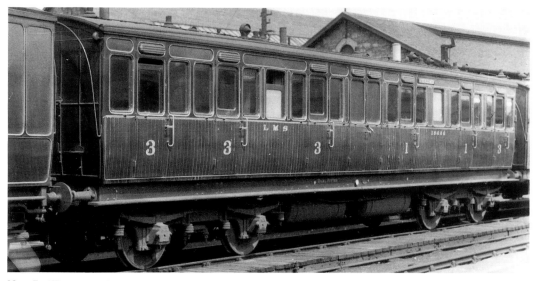

Plate 93 . Ex-HR No. 53, which was a Type J Composite built 1899 to Diagram 17. Now reliveried in full LMS passenger livery and numbered 18660. If the records are right and this *is* No. 53, this very coach was badly damaged in the Baddengorm Burn accident of 18th June 1914: see Plate 232 in P Tatlow's *Highland Miscellany*. Note that the repaired coach has a matchboard body below the waist, whereas previously it was panelled. *[HC Casserley*

NON-PASSENGER COACHING STOCK

Livery

LMS non-passenger coaching stock livery was usually similar to that applied to carriages, but often showed economies of simplification and the use of such things as pale yellow instead of gold gilt. More detail can be found in the reference works listed in the bibliography.

Renumbering

Non-passenger coaching stock was numbered by the LMS in a separate series and ex-Highland vehicles fell in the range 7364 to 7848. This included:

- Post Office vans
- full passenger brake vans
- luggage vans
- carriage trucks
- horse boxes
- open fish trucks
- valuable cattle vans.

The 1933 renumbering scheme embraced non-passenger coaching stock as well and the table below shows how the new numbers were allocated to surviving Highland stock.

Type	Second LMS Nos.
Post Office vehicles	30297/9 and 30321 to 303023
Bogie Corridor Full Brake	31952 and 32897 to 32899
Bogie Non-corr Full Brake	33692 to 33697
6-wheel Brake	34282 to 34293
Covered Carriage Truck	37189 to 37199
Luggage Van	37897 to 37899
Covered Carriage / Fish Truck	37493 to 37499
Open Fish Truck	40970 to 40998
Open Carriage Truck	41893 to 41898
Horse Box	43777 to 43792

The valuable cattle vans had been reclassified as freight stock in the meantime.

Travelling Post Offices

Ex-Highland travelling Post Office vehicles carried two royal ciphers on each side at approximate quarter points, or later only one centrally placed on the side with the mail collectors and traductor arms. Unlike other LMS TPOs, however, they did not appear to have had ROYAL MAIL emblazoned in large letters along each side until the BR era. [25]

GOODS VEHICLES

Under the auspices of the LMS up until 1936, ex-Highland wagons were painted in light grey with the owning company's initials in white across the vehicle side in large letters.

Thereafter, the colour changed to bauxite and the initials reduced in size and placed to the lower left hand corner. See the bibliography for references to further detail.

Renumbering [26]

Highland Railway goods stock was numbered in the block 292000 to 299999. Within this, it seems from the examination of photographs that the various types of vehicles were placed in blocks. Precise details are not known; however the table below shows what has been identified.

Type	LMS Nos.
Goods Brake Van	2940xx
Cattle and Sheep	2945xx
Mineral and Open	296xxx
Service Vehicle	297xxx

There were undoubtedly other groupings which have yet to be identified. Service vehicles were broken down into sub-groups and also included vehicles from other constituents of the LMS allocated to the Highland Section following grouping. Likewise, ex-HR vehicles taken into the departmental stock of another section took a number from that section's allotted series of numbers, e.g. Nos. 354398/354958 which was an ex-travelling Post Office van which saw its last days out as a tool van at Corkerhill.

British Railways employed the same numbers with the addition of the prefix M, or DM in the case of Departmental stock.

Goods Brake Vans

During the LMS period many ex-HR goods brake vans carried the following additional lettering across

---

[25]   See page 110 in Lambert's *Highland Railway Album Vol. 2*.

[26]   Further details may be found in *The Highland Railway Journal*, Vol. 1, No. 5, page 16.

Plate 94. The penultimate design of goods brake van of 20 ton, 20 feet over headstocks and steel underframe No. 294023 was photographed in the light grey livery in vogue until 1936, with large company initials in white across the body side. Note the HIGHLAND SECTION PERTH applied on the lower right.

[WE Boyd - Peter Tatlow collection

the lower right hand body side in 4 inch letters:

HIGHLAND

SECTION

and below that the van's home depot, such as:

PERTH

as can be seen in Plate 94. Later the depot only appeared, e.g. AVIEMORE/FORRES, BEITH (centrally placed), MONTROSE and ARDROSSAN (in post-1936 livery).

DEPARTMENTAL STOCK

Some Engineer's vehicles, particularly ballast wagons, bore a large **E** on the left hand side and towards the right hand end in white either an **H** or a smaller **S** over **H** with a horizontal bar between:

$$\frac{S}{H}$$

Prior to World War II at least, the 15 ton Cowans Sheldon steam breakdown crane was painted in lined out crimson lake locomotive livery and utilised coach transfers for the lettering and numbering.

LINESIDE

The Northern Division of the LMS, which embraced the former Caledonian and Glasgow and South Western railways, as well as the Highland, tended to be different from the other divisions south of the border. This was most apparent in the infrastructure in that there was little effort to show what we would now call corporate identity. Following World War II buildings were still drab with hardly any attempt

at the brown and cream which was the normal elsewhere. Hawks-eye signs were rare to the point of being non-existent in Scotland.

Station Buildings

Initially it appears the LMS continued to apply burnt-sienna and purple-brown to the timber work.

From about 1936 a much lighter shade, consistent with cream, and purple-brown were used, an early example being Tain. Not many stations were so treated prior to the outbreak of World War II and it was into the BR period before this style became universal in the Highland area, as well as the rest of Scotland, when it was accompanied by station and other name boards in white on a light blue background. If the boards were new, which they often were, they were enamelled steel plate.

Signal Cabins

The same painting schemes were used on signal cabins. The LMS's practice was to fix name boards to the ends of cabins in white on a black background. Under BR of course these also became white on light blue.

Signals

Whereas the front face of distant signal arms had been painted red with a white fish tail, from about 1926, as arms were repainted or renewed, the colour was altered to yellow with a black fish tail.

Plate 95. No. 14768 *Clan MacKenzie*, showing the pre-1928 lined red LMS passenger livery, with the name in a straight line between the splashers. *[David Jenkinson collection*

Plate 96. An example of a small Highland station in LMS days is the original Lochluichart on the Skye line, before the deviation of the line and a new station were constructed in the early 1950s, prior to raising the water level of the loch as part of the Conon Valley hydro-electric scheme. The cream upper and purple brown livery scheme has been applied to the timber buildings. LMS bill boards are apparent and the station name board has dark letters and border on a light ground. *[late Graham Langmuir - AG Ellis collection 2135*

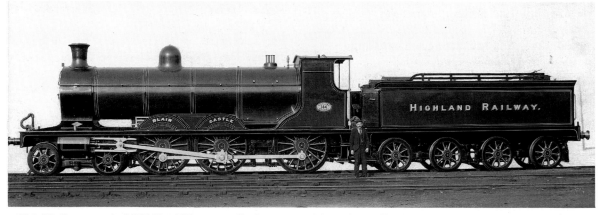

Plate 97. To contrast the full LMS and HR passenger liveries, No. 144 Blair Castle poses for the camera. *[David Jenkinson collection*

Plate 98. Pullman Sleeping Car *Balmoral* introduced to the southern main line in 1885, previously having been on Great Northern Railway east coast night trains. It and its partner *Dunrobin* were converted to 8 wheels in the early 90's, having been 6-wheeled. The livery was dark brown with gilt lining and lettering. Along with some remnants of *Dunrobin*, *Balmoral* still exists as a partial body with some interior extant, having been part of a bungalow on the South Coast for many years. In very poor condition, its future is uncertain.

[HRS collection, courtesy AJ Lambert

Plate 99. Interior of Pullman Sleeper *Balmoral*, demonstrating the day and night configurations of the seating and sleeping arrangements.

[HRS collection, courtesy AJ Lambert

BIBLIOGRAPHY

The following are significant sources of further, more detailed, information:

Highland Railway

Cormack JRH and Stevenson JL, *Highland Railway Locomotives - Book 1 - Early days to the "Lochs"*, Railway Correspondence And Travel Society, 1988.

Cormack JRH and Stevenson JL, *Highland Railway Locomotives - Book 2 - The Drummond, Smith & Cumming Classes*, RCTS, 1990.

Hunter DLG, *Carriages & Wagons of the Highland Railway*, Turntable Enterprises, 1971.

Hutchison Sir Eric AO, *The Highland Railway*, Model Railway Constructor, in 13 parts from March 1954 to March 1955.

Reed B, *Loco Profile 17 - Jones Goods & Indian L*, Profile Publications Ltd, 1971.

Stephenson Locomotive Society, *The Highland Railway Company and its Constituents and Successors 1855-1955*, The Stephenson Locomotive Society, 1955.

Tatlow P, *A History Of Highland Locomotives*, Oxford Publishing Co., 1979.

Locomotive Magazine, 1898 to 1920.

Model Railway Constructor, Nov. 74, Jan. 76, Feb. 77, Aug. 78, Mar. 80, Apr. 80, in-depth studies of some locomotive classes by E Bellass.

Mention must also be made of *Britain's Railway Liveries* by EF Carter, which, although containing comprehensive albeit unstructured information, cannot be regarded as wholly reliable since much was simply culled from other publications; it is out of print but is commonly available in libraries and has a useful colour reference chart.

Application of LMS Livery

Essery RJ and Jenkinson D, *Locomotive liveries of the LMS*, Roundhouse/Ian Allan, 1967.

Essery RJ and Jenkinson D, *The LMS coach*, Roundhouse/Ian Allan, 1969.

Essery RJ and Jenkinson D, *An illustrated history of LMS coaches*, OPC, 1977.

Essery RJ and Morgan KR, *The LMS wagon*, David and Charles, 1977.

Essery RJ and Jenkinson D, *An illustrated history of LMS locomotives - Volume one - General review and locomotive liveries*, OPC, 1981.

Essery RJ, *An illustrated history of LMS wagons - Volume two*, OPC, 1983.

Essery RJ and Jenkinson D, *An illustrated history of LMS locomotives - Volume three - Absorbed pre-group classes, Northern Division*, OPC, 1986.

Essery RJ and Jenkinson D, *An illustrated history of LMS standard coaching stock - Volume one - Non-Passenger Stock*, OPC, 1991. (Volume two due in 1995.)

Figure 40. A contemporary engraving of No. 89 *Sir George*, clearly showing the two-tone livery scheme and the layout of the lining. This engraving first appeared in *The Engineer* on 1st February 1895.   *[Reproduced courtesy The Engineer*

INDEX

ACKNOWLEDGEMENTS

The hobby as a whole is indebted to Sir Eric Hutchison and Gavin Wilson for the original collation of information. The authors also would like to acknowledge the assistance of the following Highland Railway enthusiasts who have contributed greatly over the last 20 years to both the initial, privately circulated manuscripts and this present published version: Keith Buckle, R.B. Constant, the late Dick Duffy, the late Alan Dunbar, Brian Hilton, the late James Kennedy, Eddie McKenna, Alan Payne and Alan Wright. We also gratefully acknowledge the many Society members and others who have contributed further information and material. We are especially grateful to Peter Tatlow for his input, help and guidance, tirelessly given.

Each photograph and drawing is acknowledged individually in the text. Many have been culled from the Highland Railway Society's collection, as well as members' and others own: we gratefully acknowledge each and everyone who has contributed. Permission for inclusion has been sought from the original source where possible; however, when the source is unknown or contact could not be made, then the person or organisation providing the material has been credited.

The authors and the Highland Railway Society are also pleased to recognise the role of the Historical Model Railway Society, especially that of Gerry Arundel, in enabling the book's publication through David Jenkinson's Pendragon Press. It is most unlikely that the material in this book would have been published without all three organisations working together.

The material has been substantially extended since the initial collation; any errors are the authors' alone. They would welcome any corrections and more information.

Plate 100. No. 2 *Ben Alder*, showing the Drummond I lining out extremely clearly. Note the lining around the Westinghouse pump cylinders. Note also that the cab door is not lined out on the inside. *[RK Blencowe collection 24546*

Membership of the **Highland Railway Society** is open to all with an interest in historical research or in modelling the Highland Railway, its predecessors and successors. The Society publishes a quarterly *Journal* which contains a wide variety of articles relating to the railway and which provides a means for members to exchange and seek information. There are also regular meetings in both Scotland and England, and various services and facilities are offered by the Society.

Details of membership of the Society may be obtained from the Membership Secretary: Sandy Harper, The Saplings, Weir Road, Hanwood, Shropshire SY5 8LA.

Availability of drawings: Large scale drawings of the locomotive number plates and works plates which feature in this book are available to members as part of the Society's extensive drawing service.

The **Historical Model Railway Society** was founded in 1950 to foster the research and recording of information relating to the railways of the British Isles and to make it widely available not only to those engaged in building accurate and authentic models but also to all with an interest in Britain's railway heritage. Recognition of the Society's valuable contribution in this educational field came in 1977 when charitable status was granted to it.

Members of the Society receive a high quality quarterly journal and a bi-monthly Newsletter. The Society also has extensive collections of drawings and photographs and a large library. A system of Company Stewards, each specialising in a particular company, forms a clearing house for the exchange of information and a point of contact for enquiries. Local Area Groups meet regularly and talks are given in many parts of the country.

Further information and a prospectus/membership application form can be obtained from: Historical Model Railway Society, Chaworth House, 15 Byron Gardens, Southwell, Nottinghamshire NG25 0DW.